THE FAMILY
REUNION PLANNER

◇

Also by Donna Beasley

Family Pride: The Complete Guide
to Tracing African-American Genealogy

DONNA BEASLEY

The FAMILY REUNION Planner

MACMILLAN • USA

Macmillan
A Simon & Schuster Macmillan Company
1633 Broadway
New York, NY 10019

Library of Congress Cataloging-in-Publication Data
Beasley, Donna.
    The family reunion planner / Donna Beasley.
    p. cm.
    Includes bibliographical references (p.) and index.
    ISBN 0-02-861193-4
    1. Family reunions—United States—Planning. I. Title.
GT2423.B43 1997   96-48657
394—dc21   CIP

                10 9 8 7 6 5 4 3 2 1

            Book design by Nick Anderson

                Photography credits
                Donna Beasley: page 86
        James Horn: pages i, 1, 2, 48, 74, 100 and 107
        Reunion Magazine: pages 40 and 62

        Printed in the United States of America

To my mother
for convincing me I can if I think I can.
for feeding me, when I was writing and not cooking.
for being a sounding board for my ideas.
for checking on me every day, just because she loves me.

Contents

Contents

Acknowledgments

Special thanks to Jane Crouse for her editing expertise and faith in me.

Special thanks to Emma Young, who wrote the poem "My Family" and the opening chapter rhymes for this book, for the added spice of creativity.

A resounding round of applause to the reunion planners who shared the highs and lows of reunion planning for this book: Carlotta Campbell, Deborah Robinson-Campbell, Suzanne Stantley, Juanita Ware, and Freddie Williams.

Introduction

My Family

Of all the beautiful things in the world
What is most lovely to me
Is the mothers and fathers, brothers and sisters
That make up a family.

It's the uncles, aunts and cousins
(Some live so far away).
It's the grandpas and grandmas
Who always brighten the day.

It's the cute little children
Having fun, running wild.
And the cuddly, little babies
That always bring on a smile.

And every year I look forward
To a very special time
When I will be reunited
With this family I call mine.

It's family reunion time.
The time I hold so dear.
A time that I look forward to
Each and every year.

A time to visit a new city
Or stay home and be the host
And share with my whole family
The sites and scenes I love the most.

There's lots of fun to be had,
Lots of sights to see,
But the sight I love most
Is my wonderful family.

There's good food to eat,
Lots of memories to share,
And lots and lots and lots of love
'Cause the whole family is there.

I can hold my head high.
I have a right to be proud,
'Cause this crowd I'm partying with
Is no ordinary crowd.

They're the cream of the crop,
The best there can be.
They're the folks I love the most.
They're my family.

—EMMA YOUNG

We are kin. One people, one God, one human family and one history. Our individual families are our links in the chain of life. That chain is the platform from which we launch our lives. Our family history connects us to all history. Each of us is a patch in the quilt of our family's history. The day you were born you were carefully and beautifully woven into your place of honor on the quilt. You are forever connected to your lineage, your ancestors and your family.

I am a genealogist, and I have traced my family back in time through seven generations. Genealogists preserve a family's history for future generations and keep the memory of ancestors alive in both printed words and photographs. Because of my love of family and family preservation, I am an advocate for family reunions. This is the one time of year when the family can be lifted up and celebrated. It is a time to hug relatives you rarely see, honor the elders and give thanks for the birth of new life. It is a chance to break bread and show fellowship with one another. It is a time to honor your past and celebrate your future. It is also a time to remind yourself that you are connected, and to whom you are connected.

There is much talk these days that what is wrong with America can be directly linked to the destruction of American families and traditional values. A child is lucky today to grow up with two parents, and luckier still if he or she has an extended family. But I think family is America's greatest asset. It is worth nurturing and preserving. Fortunately, a lot of other people feel the same way because family reunions have made a strong comeback.

In fact, according to *Reunion Research* Americans hold about 200,000 family reunions each year. Over seven million Americans attend these reunions. While these figures include all races and ethnic groups, there are cultural differences.

For example, African-Americans often have large family reunions with over 150 participants, according to the Family Reunion Institute at Temple University. Many African-American family reunions alternate between northern and southern cities every other year. Keeping up with relatives who have moved north and connecting with the home base in the south are common reasons African-Americans attend family reunions. They want their children to know who their relatives are.

Additionally, more African-Americans are tracing their family history. The family reunion becomes an opportunity to share family heritage from generation to generation.

Most family reunions are planned in the summer or around holidays when children are out of school. Therefore, family reunions often fuel the summer travel industry. *Black Enterprise* magazine (August 1994) reports that 45 percent of African-Americans' travel is to attend a family reunion.

So when was the last time you saw your grandmother? Or walked around the old neighborhood? Maybe, you're thinking, it's time to get the kinfolks together for a reunion. What a great idea! Family reunions strengthen our bonds of love and allow us to stay close-knit.

The purpose of this book is to guide you to create a safe, fun and wonderful reunion. This book will walk you through the many details from an auspicious start to the fabulous finish—a glorious family celebration. So come on, let the fun begin.

The Family
Reunion Planner

Many a great reunion plan
Is gone and now departed.
'Cause the family had a great idea,
But they never would get started.

THE RHYTHM SECTION

In a musical group core members make up the rhythm section. Usually the drummer, piano player, lead guitar and the musical director make up this core group. Oftentimes entertainers travel to a city bringing their rhythm section and pick up other needed musicians locally. The family reunion planning committee is the family rhythm section. These core players create the beat and pace of a joyous celebration.

Hosting a family reunion is one of life's most rewarding and challenging experiences. While it is a tough job, it is also great fun and personally satisfying. After all, planning your reunion is a gift you give to your family. There will be both moments of joy and pain; times when your efforts will be appreciated and times when the job will seem thankless. But press on, it will always be worth it. There is no right or wrong way to plan a reunion. All you need to be successful is a family.

This book provides the practical information you need to organize the event. But more than that, my goal is to provide you with creative inspiration, tried-and-true ideas from family reunion planners and worksheets to use to make the job easier. On reunion day your efforts will be rewarded by a memorable, meaningful and manageable event.

GETTING STARTED

Begin with either a telephone or written survey of family members. The purpose of the survey is to get some ideas of how your family feels about getting together. It helps you determine if out-of-town relatives would be willing to travel to the reunion. The survey provides the framework around which you'll plan your celebration. After all, your goal is to plan an event most of your family members will be eager to attend. The following is a list of suggested survey questions.

- Are you interested in coming to a family reunion?
- What month is best for you attend?
- Would you be willing to travel to (city name)?
- What activities would interest you at the reunion?
- Do you have any special talents or equipment to contribute (such as being a deejay, providing computer skills and so on)?
- Are you willing to help in the planning?

Once the surveys have been returned you'll know how to proceed; you'll get some ideas for events; and you will know who you can count on for help. The next step is to form a planning committee.

PLANNING COMMITTEE

Strive to form your committee twelve to eighteen months in advance of the reunion. The earlier you get started the more time you'll have to evaluate potential sites, raise funds and hunt down lost relatives. The first rule of planning a family reunion is to create a planning committee.

Every reunion committee needs a leader or chairperson, whose job is to coordinate details, organize the team and keep the reunion's forward momentum going. More than likely, this is your job. Keep in mind that the leader is not a dictator. Hosting a reunion is not a one-person job. Every member of the committee has an equal voice and vote in the final decisions of the group.

Don't be a lone ranger. Delegate and share the responsibilities and rewards for the event. This will create a bond among family volunteers and a sense of pride in pulling together as a team to create the reunion. By using a team approach, you can ensure that planning the reunion will be fun.

Contact several family members and ask them to be on the reunion planning committee. Hopefully some folks volunteered when you did the survey. No matter how many people volunteer, usually only three to five people will be the key worker bees and make up the core planning team. Often people will say yes, but then don't have the time because of prior commitments. Don't turn down their offers of help, even though they may not have time to focus on the big picture. Later you can give them a specific task to do after the planning committee has set the course of action for the reunion. Your core committee members are usually referred to as the host family.

Once the host family reunion committee is in place, set a date and time for your first planning meeting. At this meeting, determine what kind of family reunion you'd like to host and what kind you have the time to pull together. There are many points to consider.

- How extensive should the reunion be?
- What time of year will you host your reunion?
- Should it be one day only, like a picnic, or a full weekend?
- Is the reunion for the maternal side of the family, paternal side of the family or both?
- Are there names, addresses and phone numbers available to contact family members?
- How many family members will be invited?
- Should the reunion center around a specific theme?

Make planning the family reunion as much fun as the event. One key way is to have meetings once a month hosted by a committee member. This person prepares a meal and shares family photos or videos before and after the meeting to keep everyone in the spirit of joyous planning. Do a report of what happened at the meeting, who is responsible for what and what decisions were reached. At the next meeting, begin with the previous month's report, checking off finished projects and including upcoming ones. Besides providing good organization, this also gives the committee a sense of accomplishment.

SUBCOMMITTEES

There are many tasks associated with putting together a family reunion. To keep the burden of details off the shoulders of one individual, the workload must be shared. To do this, responsibilities should be broken down and assigned to individuals or subcommittees, who are put in charge of one aspect of the reunion. Key committee recommendations are as follows:

- **Site selection committee**   This committee is responsible for researching various hotel sites, picnic sites, restaurants and other meal sites.
- **Treasurer or budget committee**   This group is responsible for managing the reunions funds, opening a bank account for reunions assets, paying bills and keeping accurate records of expenditures. This job should go to someone with the most experience in money management and record keeping.
- **Fund-raising committee**   This committee is responsible for generating ideas to raise funds for reunion expenses. Once the fund-raising activities have been agreed upon this committee plans, coordinates and implements the various projects.
- **Correspondence committee**   This group is responsible for corresponding with relatives to keep them abreast of reunion activities. Usually this is done by mailing informational letters or flyers or by creating a family newsletter. This

committee maintains the names and addresses of family members on a database.

- **Program committee** This committee is responsible for planning and coordinating the activities that are going to be held on reunion day. This group is also responsible for developing and coordinating reunion keepsakes, such as T-shirts, group photos, program books and so on.
- **Family history preservation committee** This group is responsible for collecting and displaying family history. In its most basic form, this would include creating a family tree and displaying old family photos and any historical documents. This committee might also include a photo and brief write-up of any family member who died during the past year or any child born or adopted during the last year.

TYPES OF REUNIONS

There are many ways to conduct a family reunion. Most are one-day or weekend-long events. There are, however, notable exceptions. A friend's family recently held its reunion aboard a cruise ship. Over 100 family members enjoyed cruising the Caribbean for seven days. If you are planning your first family reunion, it may be best to keep it simple. For instance, a picnic works well.

Picnic

If a picnic site is selected, the committee will need to find out where to get a park permit, what the costs are, what dates are available and what are the best locations. Where will out-of-town guests stay? Who will provide meals? Should the meals be catered, potluck or cooked on-site by family chefs?

In my family, a picnic has always been the focus of our family reunion. I come from a large family. My mother was one of twenty children. I have sixty-six first cousins. No house could hold this group. One of my fondest childhood memories is our family reunion picnics in Chicago's Washington Park. We always held it in the same place, by the big rock. It was the only time of year when I could see most of my cousins in one place.

It was at the family reunion that I hit my first softball. We played "Piggy." The batter hits the ball and if you catch the ball it's your turn to bat. I was so proud when I caught my first ball. Since I was really small for my age, everyone moved in because they didn't think I'd hit the ball very far. My Uncle Sam was the catcher (and a great ball player). He found the lightest bat, and showed me how to hold it. He told me to choke up on it because it would give me more power for my size. Then he said, "Look out in the field. See how close up they are? They're all underestimating you because of your size. I want you to hit that ball right over their heads." Miraculously I did. No one ever underestimated me as a batter after that. And I went on as a youth to be a good hitter on my neighborhood softball team.

Making memories, influencing lives; that's what family reunions are about.

When my maternal grandparents were living we had a family reunion every year. After they died, the reunions stopped for many years. Then someone pointed out we only get together as a family at weddings and funerals. About five years ago we had one of those tough years when we had only funerals. We decided we had to stop meeting like this, and decided to reinstate the family reunion picnic. It has been a wonderful unifying experience for my family.

My brother Milton and cousin Darryll grill all the meat. Every family brings dishes that make up the rest of the menu. The food is put on the community table. Everyone is free to eat anything they want, regardless of who brought the food. We have a deejay, my cousin's husband, Bob, who plays music. As the family historian, I present the family genealogy and interview family members. We take videos and photographs and play ball. Mostly, we just have a good time.

Weekend Events

Many family reunions fill an entire weekend. Often these reunions may be hosted in different cities each year. The family members in the host city are responsible for putting together the reunion. The Robinson family reunion is held at a hotel and begins with a hospitality suite on Friday for people coming into town. Family members who live in the host city bring food to feed the traveling guests. When the event is held in St. Louis the Robinsons also have a late night excursion on the river boat on Fridays. Saturday is the family banquet. It's been held in a hotel banquet room for many years. Now, however, the Robinsons prefer to go off-site to an African-American–owned restaurant. Sunday morning they have a farewell breakfast that is casual and unstructured. Those family members who are interested go to church. At other family reunions, a minister may be brought in, and religious services, followed by breakfast, are all done at the hotel.

TIMING AND LOCATION

One of the first decisions the planning committee needs to make is to select a date and city for the reunion. If you've surveyed the family you should have some idea of what month is best for most members. You want to select a date with this time frame in mind. No doubt, there will be family members with a timing conflict. You can't please everyone. Pick a date acceptable to committee members and most family members and stick to it. By selecting your date a year in advance it will allow those with a schedule conflict time to readjust their priorities.

The following are a few other points to consider in selecting a date.

- Should the reunion coincide with a holiday?
- Should the reunion be held in the summer when most people take a vacation and children are out of school? Or

should the reunion be held during spring break or around holidays?

- During what season should the reunion be held? Should it be held in the fall or spring when hotel rates and airfares are the lowest? How about a winter reunion aboard a cruise ship or at a ski resort?

Once the date has been selected the next step is to notify family members of the city and date of the reunion. This initial mailing can be a hold-the-date postcard or a formal letter. Any correspondence should include the names of the key planning committee members and their telephone numbers.

How Often Should a Reunion Be Held?

This is a question with which reunion planners often wrestle. The timing is an individual family decision with no rule of thumb. Some families begin their reunions with annual picnics which evolve into a weekend event held every other year. My family has held a reunion picnic annually, but is now considering switching to a weekend format. Other families have reunions every two or three years.

The reasons most often given for the every-other-year format are as follows:

- To give reunion planners a break from year to year
- To allow family members to do something else with their vacation dollars during the off year
- To avoid the same old boring thing every year
- To maintain family interest and participation, especially since this generally drops after the first three or four years

The Robinson family solves this problem by switching between the three primary cities where family members reside—Chicago, St. Louis and Memphis. There is a different host committee in each city. So each team only has to plan the reunion every three years. The different city activities help keep it interesting.

The proponents of the annual reunion claim there are benefits to holding it every year. They point out the following:

- When you're first starting out, it's better to do it every year to get the family used to the idea.
- Participation builds from year to year.
- Developing the reunion as a family heritage event keeps a family's history alive and helps build a loyal following of family members who return each year. As word of mouth about the event grows, more family and friends attend.
- Family members can easily get involved during the reunion if it is an annual event. Things to do include giving relatives an opportunity to showcase their talents; allowing children an opportunity to give speeches before the group; doing something special for the elders and any parents with newborn babies. These things add excitement, generate interest and unify the family.

In the end, what you have to decide is if you and/or your committee have the drive and enthusiasm to plan the event every year. If not, the every–other or every–two–years reunion may be perfect for you.

Now that your committee is intact, the date has been selected and family members have been notified, it is time for the subcommittees to get busy implementing their various activities. In any good rhythm section, the instruments must be tuned and the band rehearsed to make good music. In the family rhythm section, committee members must develop and coordinate the activities that will ultimately culminate into the reunion symphony.

In the chapters ahead we will discuss, in detail, ideas and activities for the various subcommittees. In the next chapter, we will look at ways to handle the reunion's second greatest asset—its money.

Planning reunions can be a joy,
But you know, it's kinda funny.
Every idea we come up with
Ends up costing money.

MONEY MATTERS: FINANCING THE FAMILY SYMPHONY

Establishing and maintaining a budget is one of the essential tasks in planning a family reunion. From the very beginning there are expenses such as increased telephone bills, paper and postage. Planning committees need to set up both a separate checking account and a budget.

Even if you are planning a small reunion organized by one or two people, you still need a separate account. This will eliminate mixing your personal funds with reunion funds. Additionally, it will be easy to keep track of expenditures and pay for purchases. Many planners open a bank account in the name of their family reunion; for example, the Robinson Family Reunion. The opening deposit and purchase of checks are also early expenses.

Setting the budget may be a shared responsibility among all the committees. Each committee submits what it feels its costs will be. Managing the cash flow, keeping accurate records and tracking your reunion's financial history are the key responsibilities of the reunion planning or financial subcommittee.

SETTING BUDGETS

Setting the budget is one of the toughest challenges. But it can be simpler to do if you follow the following guidelines. There are three main areas for expenses: prereunion, reunion day and postreunion. Let's review each area.

17

Prereunion Expenses

Prereunion expenses include those discussed so far, plus deposits and costs that must be paid before the reunion. The following is a list of expenses for which you should estimate a cost.

- Telephone calls
- Postage
- Checking account and checks
- Accounting software program (such as Quicken)
- Photocopying or printing for letters, flyers and/or newsletters
- Paper and/or postcards
- T-shirts
- Welcome banner with family's name
- Hotel and/or restaurant deposits
- Park permits
- Prizes and awards
- Picnic food and supplies
- Decorations

To figure postage, multiply the number of relatives to be contacted by the number of mailings. Then multiply that figure by the cost of postage (32¢ as of this writing). You can figure photocopies the same way. For example, if you're sending a two-page notice to fifty relatives the formula will be: 50 (people) × 2 (pages) = 100 (copies) × 32¢ (postage) = $32.

Reunion Day Expenses

Reunion day expenses are those that must be paid the day of the event. These may include any balances due on any item and those participants that are paid the day they perform the service. Some potential expenses follow:

- Minister
- Disc jockey

- Photographer and/or videographer
- Speaker
- Musicians
- Beverages
- Some food items
- Generator (for picnic areas where electricity is needed for video cameras and stereo sound system)

Postreunion Expenses

Following the reunion there may be additional expenses that must be paid. Consider what these might be and include them in your budget. For example, if you hired a photographer there may be additional fees due when the photos are ready. If you then mail those photos to relatives, you'll need dollars for postage as well.

Registration Fees

Once the budget is established you can figure out what the registration fee should be per person. This money generally represents the primary base of income that will cover reunion costs. Also consider how to charge for children and senior citizens on fixed incomes.

The general rule of thumb is to keep the price for dinner banquet tickets for children and seniors down to around $10 to $15. If the banquet meal is really $20 a person, then the difference must be made up by charging more for the regular adult ticket, say $25 or $30. Or the cost could be offset with money raised by other means.

Some restaurants and hotels offer children's and/or seniors' meals for reduced rates. The site selection committee may be able to negotiate reduced children's rates for those twelve or under, and similar reductions for seniors fifty-five or older.

The following is a breakdown of the Robinson family reunion budget. It was a weekend event.

ROBINSON REUNION BUDGET	
Prereunion Expenses	
Mailings	$96
T-shirts ($6 × 50)	$300
Program booklet	$50
Car wash (soap, sponges)	$20
Car wash food for sale items (meat)	$45
Deposit for Holiday Inn	$200
Deposit for banquet	$500
Reunion Expenses	
FRIDAY	
Hospitality suite	no charge
Food (potluck)	donated
Beverages (soft drinks, beer and wine)	$50
Banquet balance at restaurant:	
75 adults @ $25 each	$1,875
18 children @ $10 each	$180
Keynote speaker	$50
Photographer	$150
Videographer	$200
Disc jockey	$100
Prizes/gifts/awards	$175
SUNDAY	
Minister	$100
Brunch (88 guests at $5 each)	$440
Postreunion expenses	None
Total Budget	$4,531

The funds to cover the Robinson reunion expenses came from a combination of registration fees, fund-raising (T-shirts and car wash) and donations from the planning committee.

KEEPING ACCURATE RECORDS

Registration fees, income from fund-raisers, sales from keepsake items and donations will be the income sources for your reunion. These funds will then be used to pay for the needed items and events before, during and after the reunion. Keeping accurate records and wise money-management tactics are important skills that will ensure a successful and hopefully profitable reunion. At the very least, you want to break even. You don't want to be passing the hat during the reunion to cover a shortfall, although there may be times when that is necessary. But good planning and good money management should get you safely to the break-even point.

The easiest way to keep track of reunion funds is with a computer. Select someone who has some financial management background, or at the very least access to a computer, to help keep track of funds and to act as the treasurer. If you are familiar with financial programs you can simply create a reunion account and keep accurate records.

If you don't have a financial program I recommend Quicken, which is available for both Macintosh and Windows applications. It is user-friendly because it works just like a checkbook. Best of all, the current cost of the software is reasonable—about $30. Quicken also makes it easy for you to create easy-to-understand budget reports for monthly committee meetings.

Even if you don't have access to a computer, you must still keep accurate records. Creating a separate bank account for family reunion records will help provide a tracking system for deposits and expenditures. The checkbook becomes the primary record of transactions, and its bottom line is the pulse of the status of your cash flow.

Purchase a ledger book from an office supply store. Keep track of all income and expenses in the ledger. This way you'll always have a permanent record. You can create a ledger book for each year. More likely, however, more than one reunion year can go in the ledger. One person should be in charge of the books. They should not wander from family to family. Too many mistakes can happen, or worse, the books may be lost. If your reunion is large and a lot of money is involved, then you may want to hire an accountant.

SEED MONEY

Every family reunion planning committee needs seed money to help finance early expenses. Additionally, reunion registrations may not cover all costs, and additional funds must be raised. There are several ways to get seed money and raise the needed money.

1. Ask reunion planning committee members to put in $20 each. This money is deducted from their registration for the family reunion.
2. Ask several family members to contribute to the event and this money can also be deducted from their registration.
3. Have a fund-raiser. The Robinson family held a car wash at a relative's gas station. They also sold hot dogs and hamburgers to waiting customers. The event was profitable and raised $248 dollars in seed money. This was more than enough to cover mailings and deposits for T-shirts. Other fund-raising ideas are described in the next section.

Fund-Raising Ideas

SELL RAFFLE TICKETS. Prizes can be donated from corporations or family members or purchased from raffle proceeds.

HOLD A BAKE SALE. If you have some good cooks in the family you can hold a bake sale at a church or take orders from co-workers and friends.

HOST A THEATER PARTY. Contact a local theater and ask if you can host a theater party. You get a group rate discount on the tickets purchased. Then you add an additional $5 or so to the normal ticket price. The group discounted amount and additional $5 become seed money.

HAVE AN AUTHOR-SIGNING OR BOOK PARTY. If you have an author in the family or have a friend who is an author, consider a book party. Buy the books at the wholesale rate from the publisher or from a local book distributor. Sell the books at the retail rate. Then invite folks over to meet the author and purchase an autographed book. You can split the income with the author or perhaps the author will donate his or her share.

HOST A SKATING PARTY. Contact a local skating rink and negotiate a price for the rink. Usually a slow night is selected. The rink will likely charge a flat fee, say $250. You get 100 tickets printed up and sell them for $10 each. If you sell them all you'll make $1,000. Deduct the cost of the rink rental and ticket printing, and the balance is your seed money. Usually the rental of the skating rink includes a disc jockey.

HAVE A CANDLELIGHT BOWLING PARTY. This is similar to the skating party except you're renting a certain number of bowling lanes. If you plan to have a huge party you may want to rent all the lanes. How many lanes you rent depends on how many people you expect to attend. There are usually four to five people per lane. If you expect 100 people, at 5 people per lane, you'll need twenty lanes. If the lane rental costs $300 and you sell 100 tickets at $10 each you'll make $1,000. Subtract the cost of the $300 lane rental and ticket printing to arrive at the amount of profit.

Bowling parties are easier to hold in the off-season (May through August) when regular bowling leagues are on hiatus. During the regular bowling season you need to be flexible in timing your event. Bowling alleys with lots of leagues may not be able to accommodate you from September through May.

One other point, candlelight bowling parties generally serve food. Depending on the bowling establishment's regulations, you can have the planning committee members bring food for a potluck or you can have the party catered. Catering, however, will eat away at your profits but it may make for a nicer event. Also, some bowling establishments don't allow outside food, and insist that all their customers buy food from certain suppliers.

SELL FAMILY COOKBOOKS. Cookbooks are common fund-raising items at reunions. Most families have some sort of food tradition. In my girlfriend Sandra's family, Aunt Dot is famous for her macaroni and cheese; Sandra is famous for her pound cake; and her mother Julia is famous for her lamb served with the mint jelly she made from the mint grown in her garden.

As an honorary member of Sandra's family, I often get the opportunity to break bread at their table. Just as in countless other families, the laughter and conversation before and after dinner are usually conducted around the table. Sharing a meal with family and friends is part of the joy of our life experience. This is carried over into the reunion experience as well. Oftentimes, recipes are shared and handed down from generation to generation.

The family reunion cookbook is an opportunity to compile these recipes to create a keepsake item for families to enjoy. Selling the book allows the reunion committee to add needed funds to its bottom line. Sources on where to get cookbooks printed can be found in the appendix.

CORPORATE SPONSORS

Soliciting corporate sponsors is another good way to raise funds. Corporations may not give you dollars but they may provide in-kind gifts, prizes, drinks or useful products. Write to corporations in the host city and request a contribution for your reunion. Let them know that both a cash donation and in-kind gifts (freebies) would be appreciated. Be sure to include information on the expected number of people attending and a reason why it would be great for the corporation to participate. Also include what the organization will get out of the experience. Perhaps you can give corporate contributors a free ad in the program booklet. It may be an opportunity to sample new products. It will be an opportunity to reward current customers and to target new customers. It's also great community goodwill.

VISITORS' CONVENTION AND TOURISM BUREAUS

A lot of assistance from the visitors' bureau in the host city is available. Like corporations, visitors' bureaus may not give you any money but they can provide other goodies. Brochures, plastic bags for T-shirts and giveaways, tourism information and historical-sites information are some of the items available from visitors' bureaus.

Passing
The
Torch

From One
Generation
To Another

Robinson Family
S T . L O U I S 1 9 9 6

I've got family here, I've got family there.
I've got family near and far.
And my challenge at reunion time
Is finding where they are.

GROUP MEDLEY

The one essential ingredient needed for a successful symphonic reunion is a family willing to play together. In music, a medley is the combining of different songs to provide a little taste of each. At the reunion, the attendees will be a medley of kinfolks who come from all over the city, the country and sometimes the world. Each will add his or her own distinctive flair to the event. Family members' attendance at the reunion must be orchestrated, from the youngest bongo to the oldest drum.

"I heard it through the grapevine" is *not* the way you want your family members to hear about the reunion. While word of mouth is a powerful communicating force, the written word is the vehicle that will provide the most accurate and detailed information. Informing these distinguished relatives and bringing them to the designated spot on the predetermined date is the job of the correspondence committee.

COMMUNICATING WITH FAMILY

Once the site and date have been selected, the correspondence subcommittee mails out the first announcement. If possible, this should be done at least a year in advance, particularly if the reunion is a weekend event. The early announcement allows people time to plan their vacations around the family reunion. Of course, that time line is not etched in stone. In 1996, my family reunion picnic was in September, and the announcement came during the first week of August.

Postcards and Flyers

An early "hold-this-date" postcard could include just the date of the reunion, the host city and the names of committee members to contact. Once the site has been selected a detailed letter or flyer should be mailed. Make sure all correspondence includes the name of the event, the theme if there is one, the place, date and cost.

A flyer should be designed in a clear, easy-to-understand format. It should also have visual appeal. Design elements like a headline in large bold print, a catchy phrase or a border can enhance reader interest in the information presented.

It is important that all telephone and written communication with family members have a feel of excitement. They need to know plans for a fun-packed "you don't want to miss this happening" is underway. The following two examples show one-page invitations that contain all the pertinent data, as well as an air of excitement.

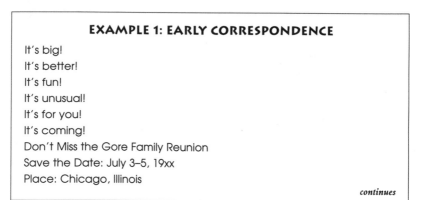

EXAMPLE 1: EARLY CORRESPONDENCE

It's big!
It's better!
It's fun!
It's unusual!
It's for you!
It's coming!
Don't Miss the Gore Family Reunion
Save the Date: July 3–5, 19xx
Place: Chicago, Illinois

continues

continued

We're currently at work planning a great event this year. Details will be sent as soon as we get them worked out. You must come! Because after all our hard work, we'll be looking forward to a hug from you. Okay don't just do it for us. Come for the food, come for the drinks, come for the camaraderie, come to see the new babies, come to toast our ancestors, come because your mother made you, just come. We guarantee you'll have a fantastic time.

EXAMPLE 2: DETAILED CORRESPONDENCE

You are cordially invited to

The Robinson Family Reunion

Our 11th Year and Growing

Our theme this year is Passing the Torch from One Generation to Another.

Don't miss this year's reunion. There will be something for everyone— entertainment, riverboats, activities for children and a special presentation of our family history.

We have negotiated a great hotel rate and reserved a block of rooms. Tell the hotel you're with the Robinson family reunion when you make your reservations. The rate is the same for single and double rooms.

Date: July 26–28

Place: Holiday Inn (Holidome) Airport

    St. Louis, Missouri

Reservations call: 800-xxx-xxxx

Special room rate: $60 per night

Time: From 5 P.M. Friday to noon on Sunday

Registration: $50 per adult

    $30 per child

T-shirts: $20 each

For more information contact: Name at 000-000-0000

Come one, come all. Show your family pride at this year's Robinson family reunion and help us pass the torch from one generation to another.

How Often Should You Correspond with Family?

In my family, we have an annual picnic and mail out one notice. A week or two prior to the event we get on the phone and call the primary family heads to remind them of the reunion date and to make sure they and their family members are coming.

For a weekend event you should plan on corresponding with your family three times before the event. Correspondence should consist of the following:

1. The early announcement, a postcard notice, should be sent months in advance as stated earlier.
2. The detailed fact sheet tells what family members should do, how much the reunion will cost and what the deadlines are for all fees. This should be sent out as early as possible, preferably eight to ten months in advance of the event.
3. The reminder notice includes all facts and deadlines, and should go out four or five weeks before the reunion.

NEWSLETTERS

Another popular form of family communication is a newsletter. A newsletter can add an element of fun and provides an opportunity to include photos and entertaining clip art (photos and illustrations with copyright clearance). The best part is that a newsletter can be a one-page fact sheet; a four-page, fact-filled report; or an eight-page, information-packed narrative. Any of these formats can have great impact. Each one can be effective and enlightening and can act as a catalyst to increased attendance at the family reunion.

There is, however, an even more important benefit to a newsletter. It is a link family members share with one another throughout the year. I have a large extended family, and most of us live in the same town. Yet, I see most of these relatives just once a year. This is also true for my out-of-town relatives. We only get together at the family reunion. Our newsletter is like a mid-year visit. It reports on family events, keeps everyone informed of the progress of the upcoming reunion and is an opportunity for family members to share their talents. Relatives can contribute poems, recipes, historical letters, current letters, photographs and more.

CREATING A NEWSLETTER

Developing a newsletter is a time-consuming process and is generally the responsibility of one person. How often you publish the newsletter should be dictated by how much time you have to donate to the project. A regular schedule is best because then the newsletter becomes eagerly anticipated. A newsletter can be produced on one of four schedules: (1) annually (once a year); biannually (twice a year); triannually (fall, winter and spring); or quarterly (four times a year).

A major factor to consider when planning a newsletter is budget. Duplicating copies and mailing newsletters can be costly. To cover expenses for the upcoming year, you might want to add a dollar to the cost of registration at this year's reunion. If you've considered the pros and cons and are still eager to start the family newsletter, here are some tips.

Get samples of newsletters other people have done. Don't limit yourself to family newsletters, get a variety. Take elements you like from the samples to develop your family's newsletter.

The best way to create a newsletter is on the computer. Don't worry if you don't have one, you can still create a great newsletter by using the local resources of a quick print shop such as Kinkos or Speedy Print. For example, Kinkos has in-house designers. You simply provide the information typed and on disk. Designers call this copy. Also give the designers your photographs or ask them to add clip art. For a fee the designers will create the newsletter. You then make copies and mail the newsletters.

The Newsletter Editor

The person responsible for creating the newsletter is the editor. Many people may contribute articles, photographs, artwork or stories. The editor, however, is generally responsible for what information is placed in the newsletter, proofreading copy and all production aspects (design, typing, layout, copying and distribution).

ELEMENTS OF A SUCCESSFUL NEWSLETTER

Masthead/Name

All newsletters have a masthead or banner at the top of the front page that shows whose newsletter it is and the date it was produced. You need to establish a name for your newsletter and then develop a masthead for the front page. This will appear on every issue. Keep the name short and catchy. When first starting out you can choose a font that is in your word processing program. You can do several things to create your own masthead with existing fonts. For instance, you can put a border around the masthead, reverse the type or enlarge the size. Or you can hire a professional to create a logo but that often is an unnecessary expense. Two examples using word processing fonts follow:

Example 1—Font: Zapf Chancery
Size: 48 points

Bass Family Quarterly

Example 2—Font: Hobo
Size: 36 points

Gore/Parker Family Gazette

Information (Copy)

The information in a newsletter should be written in a clear, understandable format. If you follow the journalist's rule of thumb, then the most important information will be in the first two paragraphs and the remaining portion of the article will add detailed information. In journalism, the most important information answers the questions who, what, when, where, why and how.

All copy can be input using any word processing program. Simply create a different file for every story included in the newsletter.

For many newsletters one person interviews family members, gets any new information, collects the appropriate photos and then writes all the copy. For other newsletters, family members submit stories, poems or information from their historical research. Either way, the information must be written or gathered. How much information is gathered determines the length or number of pages of the newsletter.

Photographs

Newsletters are generally done in black and white. Therefore, black and white photography is the easiest to work with. A four-color photograph can be used, however, particularly if you can scan it into your computer or get Kinkos or another quick print shop to scan in for you and put it on a disk. (This costs about $10.) Just remember that the photograph will print in black and white.

Clip art can also be used in place of, or in addition to, photographs. Most computers have some form of clip art that comes with the computer or is found in word processing or graphic design programs. If yours does not, you can purchase clip art from an office supply or software retailer. Two examples of clip art are shown. Exhibit 1 can be used to announce the arrival of a new baby. Exhibit 2 can be used to celebrate family members' birthdays for the month.

Exhibit 1: Baby announcement

Exhibit 2: Birthday greetings

Paper

Using white paper is standard. It also keeps expenses low. You can print your newsletter on colored paper if you think it will add impact, or just because you want to put a little color in your family's day. You can also buy paper that is preprinted with splashes of color. You make your master newsletter on white paper and then take it to a quick copy shop and have it copied onto the special newsletter paper. One source for colorful newsletter paper is Paper Direct. Call 800-APapers to order a catalog.

Number of Pages

Once the information is gathered, determine how many pages to use and how much space there is for all the information. Most newsletters are two, four or eight pages. If you're doing a two-pager you simply use the front and back of an 8½″ × 11″ paper. If you have enough copy for a four-page newsletter, take four 8½″ × 11″ pages to the print shop. Your newsletter will be printed on the front and back of paper that is 11″ × 17″. This is then folded in half, creating a four-page format. For an eight-page newsletter, the four-page format is simply done twice. The second folded page is inserted into the first. For additional fees, the printer can fold, collate and staple the newsletters together.

Design

Besides word processing, another way to create a newsletter is with graphic design. If you have access and basic knowledge of how to use Pagemaker, Microsoft Publisher or Quark software you can have greater flexibility in your newsletter design. These programs come with templates (a framework) for newsletters that make it easy to create interesting design elements like borders, wraparound type, photos and clip art. Also there is increased flexibility when using photographs.

The programs are expensive ($500 or more), so you probably won't want to purchase them unless you'll use them on a regular basis. But I often go to Kinkos and similar copy shops and use their computers for the final production of flyers and newsletters. I take my copy on disk and any photos I need scanned. Scans at Kinkos average around $10 so I only use one or two per newsletter. They have all the software I need. Plus I like to print out my newsletter on Kinkos's printer. It is a 600 dpi (dots per inch) laser printer, which makes a wonderful, clear master from which I make my photocopies.

The cost of my newsletter, which includes the computer rental time, one scan and the printout, averages about $50. Then the copies must be made for an additional cost. If you choose this format be sure to include both the production cost and the expense of duplicating copies in your budget.

If this is too expensive for you, stick with designing the newsletter in your word processing program and using clip art instead of photographs.

Type

Play around with using different type sizes and styles (fonts). Don't use too many typeface groups in your newsletter or it will look junky. Generally one or two type groups is all you need. Most copy for newsletters is done in the font Times Roman. This is similar to the type used in most newspapers. But the masthead and headlines can use a different type style or just be bolded or enlarged in the same type style. The type style you use is limited only by the number of fonts that came with your word processing or graphic design program.

TELEPHONE

Most communication with family members will be through the mail. However, reminder phone calls of final deadlines for fees are also needed. Some people forget, others need encouragement to attend and still others can't find the form you sent. Attendance at the reunion is often greatly improved by placing reminder phone calls. Divide up your list of relatives among the host committee members. Make committee members responsible for calling each relative on their list at least once following the mailing of the last written correspondence and at least two weeks prior to final due dates. This will help ensure both that your relatives attend and that the needed funds are received in a timely manner.

I scribbled Aunt Gert's number
On the back of a bill,
Wrote cousin Joe's on a place mat.
I've got my stuff together.
I just don't know where it's at.

KEEPING RECORDS: HOW TO AVOID SINGING THE BLUES

Record keeping is often an area where reunion planners sing the blues. Many are too lenient because they don't appreciate the benefits associated with good record keeping. They also don't have an easy work method.

WHY KEEP GOOD RECORDS

Keeping good records will make the job of reunion planning easier from year to year. The information is always available, and copies can be shipped from the current year's reunion planning committee to next year's committee.

Accurate records also provide a system on which to build a reunion history. This gives you more clout when you negotiate rates with hotels, approach corporations for freebies and solicit extras from local convention and tourism bureaus. Accurate records give you the data to back up your claims.

You can't negotiate very well from a position of weakness. A reunion planner can tell a hotel manager, "We expect 150 people, but we can't be sure who's coming; and we don't know how many hotel rooms we'll need. So just give us a small block." Who will take you seriously with that platform?

It's far better to negotiate from a position of strength. A well-prepared reunion planner can tell the hotel, "We have had over

150 people attend our reunion for the past three years. Fifty percent of attendees are from out of town and rent thirty-five to forty hotel rooms per reunion. Plus all 150 relatives attend the banquet." This reunion planner is in a much more powerful position to negotiate a good room rate, meal charge and other hotel perks.

Good record keeping also lets you know if your reunion is losing money, breaking even or making a profit. Orderly records make it easy to get out a mailing or make a change of address or telephone number. The bottom line is that good record keeping provides an important monitor of your reunion's performance.

"I'm not good at keeping records," you say? Don't worry. There's no need to get fancy; just keep it simple. With a minimum of time and effort you can establish an easy, workable record-keeping system.

RECORD-KEEPING SYSTEMS

The two most popular ways of keeping reunion records are on 3″ × 5″ index cards or in a computer database system. I recommend you use a paper system even if your information is on the computer. Get a three-ring binder to record the information. If your data is stored on your computer, simply print it out and keep a hard copy in the binder. This printout keeps you from having to turn on your computer each time you need to check a relative's record. Plus, it is a backup in case of a tragedy, like accidentally hitting the computer's delete button and wiping out half the addresses.

The minimum information to record is each family's name, address, telephone number and the names of all the relatives in the household. This provides the basics. More details can also be gathered, such as ages, special skills and special needs (for example, wheelchair access needed).

The information should be typed or computerized. In this information age at least one family member will have access to a typewriter or a computer. If not, type the information on one of the computers at the library. They are usually free to use. If you can't type, use lined notebook paper in the binders. Whatever system you use, leave a couple of lines under each name for notes or use the back of the index cards. An example of a basic data card is shown below.

Family _____

Registration paid?   Yes _____   No _____
Date _____   Amount _____ .
No. of adults _____   No. of children _____
Banquet tickets: No. of adults _____
                         No. of children _____
T-shirts: No. of adult _____
              Large _____   X-Large _____   XX-Large _____
              No. of children _____
              Small _____   Medium _____   Large _____
Will rent hotel room?   Yes _____   No _____

The following example shows how the form is completed.

Family <u>Brian and Catherine Armstrong with children Michelle, Donnie and Brandi</u>
Registration paid?   Yes ___X___   No _____
Date ___April 6, 1996___   Amount ___$175.00___
No. of adults ___2___   No. of children ___3___
Banquet tickets: No. of adults _____2_____
                         No. of children _____3_____
T-shirts: No. of adults ___2___
              Large _____   X-Large ___2___   XX-Large _____
              No. of children ___3___
              Small ___1___   Medium ___1___   Large ___1___
Will rent hotel room?   Yes ___X___   No _____

As you can see, no bookkeeping knowledge is required. This basic system will help you keep track of reunion registrations that come in, who is attending, if they will attend the banquet and how many hotel rooms family members will rent. Also at the end of the reunion, you can ask the hotel to give you a count of the rooms rented. From that list and your master bill (which includes banquet cost) you can tell how much revenue you represented for the hotel. That information provides your position of strength during negotiations for the next family reunion.

MAILING

Once your newsletter, flyer or family letter is done, the next step is to get it in the mail. I have found that Avery mailing labels are the best ones to use. They come in a variety of sizes and styles to fit almost any system. I recommend two ways to handle your mailing list. If you don't have access to a computer, then you will be typing or handwriting your list. If you're able to computerize your list, then you'll need database management tips.

Typed or Handwritten Mailing Labels

Simplicity is the key when getting out the mail. Therefore, good list management is essential. When it comes time to mail to relatives three or four times a year, you don't want to have to retype the list. You do want to create a master mailing list for your first mailing. From then on, only the names of new family members should be added. At the end of the reunion, the list should be saved for the next year.

The simplest way to keep track of your list is to purchase Avery labels. You can get them at any office supply store, and often at drug and convenience stores. They come in a variety of colors but white is the most popular. Just type or write an address on each peel-and-stick label on the sheet.

Stop! At this point do not peel and stick any labels to envelopes. This first label set becomes your master. Once you have the master, go and make three clear copies of it. File two copies and give the third copy to a relative as a backup for safe keeping. Now, you can peel and stick the labels onto the envelopes or newsletters for your first mailing. The next time you have a mailing simply pull out the master list from your file and copy it onto the peel-and-stick labels. Add any new names, make three copies of all new information and add that to your files.

Computerized Mail List Management

Computer software database programs streamline the challenging tasks of getting a large mailing out quickly. Inputting all the names and addresses into the database program is the simplest way to manage mailings. Plus, you can print the list out in a variety of formats: mailing and shipping labels; a list of family members' names and addresses to be included in the back of the reunion day program book; or for envelopes and index cards.

While almost every database system will work, I recommend My Advanced Mail List. The program is so easy to use that you can learn the basics in five minutes. Yet it is powerful enough to keep track of up to 30,000 names. You can sort your list alphabetically, by city, by zip code or several other options. My Advanced Mail List is available at most office supply stores, Best Buy and other retailers, or call the company direct at 800-325-3508. The program is available in Macintosh, DOS and Windows formats and costs around $30.

Postage

Postage is based on weight. At this writing, a two-page letter costs 32¢ to mail first-class but a four-page newsletter costs 55¢ to mail. If, however, the four-page newsletter is folded a second time so it is $5^1/2'' \times 8''$, then it can be mailed for 32¢.

Mail all your correspondence first-class. Remember, if you're mailing a large envelope, over $6^1/8'' \times 11^1/2''$ or over $^1/4''$ thick, there is an additional charge. Postcards cost 20¢ to mail at the time of this writing. Whatever the cost, it should be figured into your reunion budget.

Stay away from odd-sized envelopes; they slow the mail down. If, however, standard envelopes stifle your creativity and you just must be a little odd, be sure to mail early.

Where will we go?
What sights shall we see?
Where will the family meet?
These are burning questions.
But the one you'll hear most is
"What are we going to eat?"

ORCHESTRATING THE REUNION

Orchestrating the reunion can be challenging. Everything must be arranged and organized to achieve the desired harmonizing effect. Many details must be attended to for a successful reunion.

One of the early decisions is to determine the type of reunion. If it's a picnic, then it is a lot simpler to plan than a weekend event; but the details of the picnic must still be worked out. If the reunion is a weekend-long event, then the site, theme, program, housing, music and more must be worked out.

The first part of this chapter details the things you should consider if you're planning a picnic-only reunion or a picnic during your weekend event. The second part of this chapter details the things to consider for a weekend-long reunion, with the emphasis on working with hotels. The following chapter discusses the reunion program—regardless of whether it is a picnic or a weekend-long event.

ORGANIZING THE PICNIC

The key things to consider when organizing a picnic are the site, parking, weather, music, food, activities and cleanup.

Site

Most picnics are held in public parks or forest preserves. Many parks require a site permit. In Chicago, there is a race to get the best sites on the most favorable days, such as on a holiday weekend. To get a premiere summer date for a Chicago-area forest preserve, it is best to apply for the permit in January. Early application is usually a good idea, regardless of your location.

Many public parks don't require a permit. A family member or two should be assigned the job of arriving at the park early and staking and claiming a good site. These early arrivals can put up a family-reunion sign, set up the grill, lay out blankets, and generally get things started.

The site selection team should pick three park sites and visit them before making a decision on where to host the reunion. Don't just pick any park; consider the needs of your family.

- Is it accessible by bus? By wheelchair?
- Is there plenty of parking?
- How close are the restrooms? If there are none, you'll need to rent a portable toilet or two.
- Are facilities available for activities such as baseball or soccer? Is there enough space for sack races and other fun activities? Is there a beach or playground nearby for the children? Is there a lake or river nearby for boat rides?
- Is there a covered shelter in the event of rain and where everyone can congregate?
- Are there trees for shade so everyone is not baking in the hot sun?
- Are grills allowed?
- Are there plenty of picnic tables or spaces for blankets?
- Is electricity available or will a generator need to be rented?
- Has the park been sprayed for mosquito and other pest control?
- Is there security on patrol on weekends?

- Is a permit required? If so, when is the earliest you can apply? And who is responsible for getting the permit?

Parks and forest preserves are not the only places to have a reunion. The old family farm or a relative's estate may be a good place. A historical site, an amusement park or a zoo can also be a fun option.

Music

Music keeps the reunion lively. If you have family members in a band, ask them to perform. If not, draft the family deejay or hire a professional. Play fun, upbeat music. A picnic is not a place for the classics.

Also consider having a place to dance or even a dance contest. Since this is a family affair, allow the children to dance with the adults. It's a lot of fun, and it can create some great photo opportunities.

Food

What would a reunion be without food? The easiest way to handle food is to tell every family to bring its own picnic lunch. Each family can set up its own area, and folks can visit and eat from table to table. A potluck meal is, however, more fun and creates family unity around the food. With a potluck meal each family is responsible for bringing at least one thing in a large enough quantity for the whole group. The food is put on picnic tables and anyone can eat anything on the tables. There should also be people responsible for bringing cold beverages, including soft drinks and beer.

Assign a person to coordinate the potluck meal. You don't want to have ten bowls of potato salad. And you don't want what we had at one of my family reunions—a table full of meat including hamburger, hot dogs, chicken, ribs and smoked turkey, with only one side dish of potato salad. You want to be sure that a variety of food will be available. So assign people a dish to bring. Most will do it joyously. Also, many relatives have a specialty. Encourage them to bring their dish. For those relatives not known for their cooking, have them bring other things like prepared snacks, beverages or a family reunion cake (ordered from a local bakery). Everyone can bring something.

One option is to have the reunion committee provide the meat, such as grilled hot dogs, hamburgers and chicken. Family members bring side dishes and paper goods.

If no one wants to cook, and you have the budget, you can always have the picnic catered. Food such as chicken and ribs can be picked up from a fast-food restaurant, and salads can be ordered from a delicatessen.

Don't forget to have someone bring the plastic and paper goods. Plastic forks and knives, napkins and paper plates, towels and cups should be available in abundance. Also, remember garbage bags.

A reunion cake makes a nice centerpiece on the picnic table. The cake can be decorated with the name of your reunion, ancestor names or a family tree.

Activities

A well-run reunion picnic includes family, food and fun. You want people to leave happy and connected to one another. Planned activities are a good way to do that. A few suggestions follow:

PRIZES. At my family reunion some of my cousins gave a number to every adult who attended. About halfway through the picnic the numbers were called. Each winning number received an envelope. If the envelope had more than $1, then the money was the prize. Most of the money envelopes had $2 to $5 in them.

If an envelope had only $1 in it, then the winner got to pick a colorfully wrapped prize. The prizes were inexpensive things such as notepads, matches, pencils and so on. But the fun was big-time. We cheered and hollered as if we were winning big lottery prizes. We all wanted to win. What really made it great was there were enough envelopes for every adult to win something.

PONY RIDES AND/OR LARGE INFLATED TENT. Fun children's activities will make the reunion special for the youngsters. Horses have nearly mass-appeal. Those large inflated tents—with and without balls—are great for children of all ages. They love to bounce and flop about in the tents.

BINGO. Play bingo using the family name such as A. Bass or J. Gore. Create your own bingo cards.

BABY PHOTO CONTEST. Have one to several pictures of babies and give a prize for the first person to correctly name the infant(s) in the photo(s).

I'm the editor for my family's newsletter. On the front of the reunion day issue I ran a baby photo contest. I placed a little-seen photo of two children on the front page. The first person to guess the identity of the children won a prize.

This contest added an element of fun as my aunts, uncles and cousins tried to figure out who were the babies in the picture. It was a photograph of my twin cousins Lorraine and Loretta, who are now grown with children of their own. Several people hinted who they were; some guessed but wavered; but only one person claimed it definitely to win the prize (an autographed copy of one of my books).

FAMILY HERITAGE SEGMENT. This staged event could include a speech and/or toast to honor and pay tribute to the family's ancestors or elders.

ELDERS TRIBUTE. This is an award given to the oldest members of the family.

PHOTOGRAPHS. Don't forget to have someone taking photos at the reunion. If possible, have a few relatives bring their video cameras as well.

T-SHIRTS AND HATS. Have family members purchase a hat or T-shirt with the family name and reunion date.

KEEPSAKES. These may include a copy of the family genealogy, a newsletter filled with family news from around the country or someone with an instant camera taking photos. This last option is especially nice for children.

Cleanup

Keep America beautiful! Don't leave food and trash in parks and forest preserves. Recruit volunteers or assign a crew to make sure that all trash is placed in receptacles or hauled away. Always completely extinguish coals in any barbecue grills.

THE WEEKEND REUNION

As noted, there are many elements that must be coordinated to create a successful reunion. For a weekend event, site selection is the most important element.

Selecting a Hotel

The number of hotels to select from is limited by the price family members are willing to pay. Most reunions are held in mid-price hotels where the room rate is $50 to $75. The hotels are not usually located downtown but are in suburban and small-town communities.

Deborah Campbell, a member of the Robinson family reunion committee, says, "We've tried a variety of hotels, some a little more upscale than others. But we find that a Holiday Inn with a Holidome works best for us. It's a place where the kids can swim, and they have a game room. They [Holiday Inn] seem more open to things for kids. At our reunion we want both the adults and the kids to have a good time."

Freddie Williams, one of the coordinators of the Bass family reunion, says, "We prefer a mid-range hotel under $60; so we generally stay in locations away from the city. The only exception was when we held the reunion in Orlando where we were in the more popular area. However, people didn't seem to mind paying the $108 per room because of the location. Any facility we select must have a banquet hall. We also negotiate with the hotel for a free meeting room once or twice during the weekend for hospitality type events."

Williams makes an important point. It has been my experience in planning events that location greatly influences attendance. New Orleans, Orlando, Chicago and Atlanta are some of the cities that tend to draw excellent crowds.

Never, never, never book a hotel without someone from the committee conducting an on-site visit.

Negotiating with the Hotel

Once a hotel has been selected the planning committee should negotiate the contract. If possible, negotiate from a position of strength as discussed in chapter 4. Have a clear idea of what you want and what you're trying to get for your family. Prioritize your list, and take it to the meeting. At the bargaining table everyone is trying to get the most for their side. Remember, however, the best deal is one in which both sides feel they got a good deal.

Number of Rooms

Many reunions book a block of rooms. These rooms are held for family members. Never collect the money or reservations for the hotel. Let family members make their own reservations directly with the hotel. Try to negotiate so that there is no penalty for canceling any of the held rooms. This is important if attendance is unexpectedly low. If there is a penalty make sure you know what it is.

A recommended option is to not guarantee a certain number of rooms. Again, let people make their own reservations. You negotiate based on an estimate of how many rooms were rented the previous year, without a guarantee. If this is your first weekend reunion, do not guarantee rooms.

Be clear on the number of rooms that must be rented to maintain the group rate. If you go under that number your group will have to adjust the rate. A hotel may not be able to negotiate a lower room price with you. But maybe you can get a trade-off, like free continental breakfast, hospitality suite, welcome party or parking discount. Try to get a free room for every fifteen to twenty rooms rented. These free rooms can be provided to committee members, given to someone who can't afford the rental rate or awarded to the oldest relatives. You need to take into account the total hotel package when determining if you're getting a good deal.

Remember, you pay for hotels by the night. You pay for cruises by the day, including the day you arrive and the day you leave.

Points to cover when negotiating with the hotel:

1. Begin your inquiry with group reservations at the hotel.
2. Room rates—be sure to get a flat rate for the room. Don't agree to one rate for a single and a different rate for double or triple occupancy.
3. Try to get a free room for every fifteen rooms rented.
4. Negotiate a continental breakfast and a discount on parking if possible.
5. Banquet—request meal packages for both sit-down and buffet-style meals. Be sure to get the price sheet to compare cost options. Also, ask how much tax and gratuity is charged

per meal. This can add as much as 25 percent to your final bill and has pushed many a reunion over budget.

6. Public Address (P.A.) System—confirm it's included in the banquet-room rate.

7. Get the hotel's toll-free (800) phone number and request return postcards if available.

8. Phone blocks—check if it's possible to get the hospitality phone blocked from making outside hotel calls. This will prevent family members from using the hotel phone to make long distance calls and sticking the reunion committee with the bill.

9. Federal Express your contract back to the hotel so you have a signature and confirmation it was received. More about this follows in the contract section.

10. Go to the meeting prepared. Have an idea of how many rooms and meals your reunion can deliver.

Banquet

If you are going to hold your banquet in the hotel, review the menu. Family-style meals are usually the most affordable. Family-style means that the food is put on the table and the dishes are passed around by the guests. There is usually more of a variety of food choices this way.

Traditional style means that a waiter or waitress serves each person. Those attending the reunion can pick their choice of entree (usually chicken, beef or fish) when they send in their registration form. Be sure to have a vegetarian option.

Most reunions charge a cheaper price for children's meals. This may mean charging more for the adult meals to offset the loss on the children's meals.

Banquets often have centerpieces for the table. Check with the hotel to see if it has something you can use. You don't want to spend limited reunion funds on table decorations. Another option is to go for a tasty centerpiece. Pick a dessert that can act as a centerpiece until it's time to cut it. Check with the banquet manager.

Not every banquet or welcoming event is held in a hotel. The Robinson family reunion often holds its banquet at a black-owned restaurant away from the hotel. Campbell says, "We tend to enjoy the restaurant more. People are more relaxed. A hotel banquet is more formal and people tend to be on their best behavior while wearing their best clothes. Even the food is more fun in the restaurant, and tends to have a distinctive African-American flair. Down-home cooking, just like mom's."

Williams says, "At our last family reunion we held our welcome event in the church banquet hall. The local family members brought in the food and the church let us use the facility at no charge. It was a low-cost but fun get-acquainted night."

Contract

I've heard a horror story or two about problems with the hotel contract. Here are some points to keep your contract problem-free. Once the contract is agreed upon put down a deposit of $50 to $100. Pay by check or get a receipt. If you mail your signed contract back to the hotel, send it via overnight service or certi-fied mail so there is a signature confirming receipt. If you hand-carry the signed contract to the hotel, take two copies and have someone from the banquet staff sign and date the copies verify-ing receipt. This way if the hotel is overbooked it can't say it never got your contract. That is exactly what happened to a high school when its senior class arrived for prom night. Its party room had been given away! In fact, to protect yourself from over-booking it's a good idea to put in the contract that your group has first access to available rooms.

Be sure to include a cancellation clause for disasters, diseases or a hotel that is not in proper condition. If your reunion is to be in a Carolina coastline town, for example, you'll want to be able to cancel without a problem if a hurricane leaves the hotel damaged or the area looking like a disaster zone.

While negotiating the contract write down those points that you and the hotel agreed upon. When you get the contract, you'll have a handy checklist to which to refer. If there is a discrepancy or if you don't like the contract, don't sign it. Go back to the bargaining table.

Liability

All the reunion planners I interviewed told me they had a hospitality, meet-and-greet event on the first night of the reunion weekend. It was usually potluck with relatives bringing the food. No one realizes that if something goes wrong, such as food poisoning, you and the committee are personally liable—not the hotel. The same is true of alcohol. The best way to protect yourself is not to bring food and drink into the hotel. Try to negotiate a welcome party into your contract. Let the hotel provide food and drink and handle all liability. Family members can bring food to the picnic.

In the United States we have a law that public places must be wheelchair accessible. Make sure the hotel you book has complied.

Notifying the Family

Once the hotel has been selected it will give you a toll-free number for family members to call and make reservations. Sometimes hotels also give postcards or brochures to send to family members to tell them something about the facility. The correspondence going to family members should include the reunion location, dates, toll-free number and a committee contact person.

Once the hotel has been selected the next challenge is to develop the program.

Everything won't be perfect,
No matter how hard you plan.
But you can take pride
In the fact that you tried.
'Cause a "try" and "success" go
hand in hand.

ARRANGING THE MUSICAL SCORE

All music is sound but not all sound is music. It takes the right arrangement, the correct blend of notes to give music just the right "swing." It is that correct blend or rhythmic flow you seek as you plan and organize the activities of your reunion. Most weekend-long reunions are organized around four events: welcome party on Friday night; Saturday picnic; Saturday night banquet dinner; and farewell breakfast or church service on Sunday. Some folks choose to skip the picnic and have a banquet only. This leaves Saturday free for sightseeing or conducting family-oriented seminars. If you're planning a weekend-long reunion, it's a good idea to organize your reunion around a theme. The following are a few suggestions from reunion planners.

REUNION AND BANQUET NIGHT THEMES

FAMILY LINKS. Create chain links on your invitation and the front of your program books. Inside, put a quote such as, "Each of us is a link in our family's chain, and when united we stand strong. You're invited to bring your link and unite with your family at this year's reunion."

UNITING YESTERDAY, TODAY AND TOMORROW. The Bass family reunion committee divided the family into age groups and had a seminar for each group. For example, they had a rapping with the elders seminar, an exhibit highlighting treasured memorabilia and an "All About Me" session to show children how they fit onto the family tree.

PASSING THE TORCH FROM ONE GENERATION TO THE NEXT. This Robinson family theme centered on the younger members understanding the importance of family and their responsibility to its preservation.

You can also select a few fun themes.

COMEDY. This is a great theme if you have a few comedians or would-be comedians in the family. You could include jokes or riddles on the invitation and within the program book. During the entertainment portion of the banquet, have family members tell their favorite jokes. Be sure to include the children; they're bound to know a few knock-knock jokes.

Have someone imitate a comedian from the present, like Sinbad; or the past, like Moms Mabley or Richard Pryor. Keep it clean; after all it is a family affair.

COSTUMES. Instead of dressing up for the banquet, people can wear clothes from a particular period. Do you remember bell bottoms and platform shoes? What about the period when we shouted "I'm Black and I'm proud"? The slogan was made popular by the James Brown song. You remember the period when black was beautiful and we no longer allowed people to call us Negroes, when we sported dashikis, wore big naturals and carried afro picks? You probably know relatives who still have those old clothes hanging in their closets. This is the time to wear them.

MOTOWN OR SOLID GOLD THEME. This theme borrows music from the 1950s, 1960s and 1970s. Relevant song titles from the period can create your theme, with a small excerpt of the song's words appearing on the invitation and in the program book. "We Are Family," made popular by the singing group Sister Sledge, and "Family Reunion," sung by Lou Rawls, are examples. If yours is a picnic event, try "Stone Soul Picnic" by the Fifth Dimension or "Hot Fun in the Summertime" by Sly and the Family Stone.

Have a few special guests show up. My church had an after hours fund-raiser where a James Brown imitator stole the show. Diana Ross is another fun person to imitate, as she throws back her head, uses her hand to toss her hair and says "I love you, I love you" while blowing kisses to the crowd—all while singing "Reach out and touch somebody's hand, make this world a better place if you can."

FAMILY HISTORY. This is a celebration of your family's heritage. Have family members bring old photo albums or historical family photos to share. Have the family griot, or the oldest family members, tell the history. Consider having a knowledgeable person speak from each generation. Each speaker is bound to describe the family history differently but the variety will give a rounded richness to your family's story. If you're lucky enough to have a genealogist or family historian in the family, let him or her make a formal presentation. Or designate a keynote speaker to portray someone from history such as poet Phyllis Wheatley, author Langston Hughes or abolitionist Harriet Tubman, or to read exerpts of their writings during the event. The more family members involved, the more historic figures can be imitated.

One variation on this theme is the great debate. Two people represent the opposing viewpoints of an issue or approach and argue the merits of each side. A popular debate subject is "different approaches to the same dream," with Booker T. Washington and W. E. B. DuBois debating, or Martin Luther King and Malcolm X facing off. This can also be done with women in history.

You may also consider hiring an actor or actress. Check community theater groups. Also, some historical societies have actors play characters from history during special programs. Contact the societies to see if they have a recommendation.

AFRICAN MOTHERLAND. This theme celebrates both African and American culture. Invitations can have an African border or contain an African proverb, such as "It takes a whole village to raise a child." On banquet night everyone can wear outfits that reflect African culture. The beauty of the fabrics' colors, unique hats and diversity of clothing will add a touch of high drama to the event. You could even include a fashion show featuring adults and children. Alternately, a fashion show for children only could be called Kente Kids, which lets the children show off their outfits.

The keynote speaker could act the part of Nelson Mandela, giving a talk on the changes in South Africa and reading excerpts from Mandela's book. The program announcement would read, "Michael Johnson presents an evening with Nelson Mandela."

POLITICAL CONVENTION. This is an enjoyable event we've conducted at my church. The idea is to create an air of excitement much like that at a Democratic or Republican convention. Signs and a cheering crowd for the candidates are needed. During my church event each candidate was allowed to give a ten-minute talk on his or her platform. There was the candidate for love, the candidate for peace and the candidate for prosperity, to name a few. Each speech had some really good points and an element of fun. At your family convention your candidates' platform could be for family unity, kid power, forgiveness or honoring ancestors.

You could, of course, poll the popularity of candidates by letting the crowd vote with its applause. The candidate with the most applause wins. Or, you can declare every candidate a winner and applaud them all.

The themes suggested here are only the beginning. Be creative and use the talent in your family to create a theme everyone will appreciate.

ENTERTAINMENT
Banquet Speakers

Consider having a keynote speaker. Speakers can be found by contacting local genealogy clubs or historical societies. If there is an African-American museum in the reunion city, it may know of a speaker to contact. Often these people will speak at no or low cost.

Banquet speaker suggestions include:

1. Authors who have written on subjects of interest to African Americans. For example, Glenette Tilley Turner, author of *Running for Our Lives,* and Sharon Draper, author of *Lost in the Tunnel,* have both written children's novels with the Underground Railroad as their themes. Their insight on the subject could make an interesting talk. These particular authors are based in Chicago and Cincinnati, respectively. When planning your reunion look for authors in your area. check local genealogy clubs or community librarians for suggestions.

2. Professors of Black History Studies can also make great speakers. A potential topic could be the "Evolution of the Black Family from 1960 to the year 2000." Check with local colleges for recommendations.

3. Comedians add a lighter touch and can be fun speakers. Pick one that can tell jokes around a family theme. Contact a local theater group or comedy club for recommendations.

Music

Be sure to hire a deejay. Make sure he or she brings a sound system and the kind of music you want played. A good price for a deejay is $25 per hour. Local nightclubs are good sources for deejays.

Photographs

Consider hiring a professional photographer to take pictures of family groups. Also, one of those large panoramic photos may be fun to have as well. For more information contact Panoramic Photography, 7315 Lake Shore Drive, Cedar Lake, Indiana 46403, or call 800-642-4686.

Workshops/Seminars

Some families skip the reunion picnic, preferring to have workshops and seminars on Saturday. These seminars are designed to provide insight into family history and promote interaction among family members. They should be enjoyable to attend.

Freddie Williams, who started the first Bass family reunion, has graciously agreed to allow one of her family's reunion workshop series to be reprinted in this book. The program series was selected because it demonstrates creativity, promotes family history, honors the contributions of African-Americans to building a strong country and preserves the family's oral history. Plus, there was something for all age levels. The workshop series follows.

Workshop 1: Rapping with the Elders

This session is designed to provide insight into our family history from a living source. Elder family members including Mrs. Amelia Gossett, Orlando, Florida; Reverend James Bass, Chicago, Illinois; and Mrs. Lucille Brown, Detroit, Michigan, will be available to answer your questions. You are encouraged to bring your camcorders, cameras, tape recorders, pens, pencils and inquisitive minds.

Workshop 2: Tripping Through the Archives: Traveling Through the Years with the Basses

Treasured memorabilia from family members will be available for viewing. Highlights of this exhibit are photos from past family reunions dating back to the 1970s. Family members are encouraged to share family anecdotes and memories of their favorite reunion in the memory box. These memories will be published in future yearbooks.

Workshop 3: Honoring Our Ancestors: "We Benefit from Their Ceaseless Struggles"

A family member who has been researching the Bass family will share her insights and encourage you to start your own research. A booklet containing a mini-history and "how-to forms" for genealogy research have been prepared for this session. History buffs and those interested in the Bass family history are encouraged to attend. Freddie Williams (Chicago) is the group leader.

Workshop 4: Viewing Our Past

Home movies and videos of early reunions will be shown. Come and see yourself and other family members when everyone was much younger. Films from as early as 1970 are available.

Workshop 5: Chit 'n Chat (Sip 'n Nip)

Family members ages twenty to thirty-five years old will meet and chat while dipping into delicious munchies. This session is designed as a fun activity for our young adult family members to get to know each other and to establish their relationship to Sam and Amelia Bass.

Workshop 6: Rolling Along with the Basses

Members fourteen to twenty years old are invited to roll along with the Basses at the Maywood skating rink from 8 P.M. to 11 P.M. Free bus transportation provided. In-transit family members along with their newfound cousins are encouraged to meet and establish their connections to Sam and Amelia Bass. Parents are totally responsible for participants in this activity, which is available only to the specified age group.

Workshop 7: All About Me: Bass Youth/Our Future

This session is designed for ages eight to thirteen years to explore where their leaf hangs on the family tree and to meet other relatives in their age range. Discovery of this theme will be made through discussion, fun and games. A special workbook has been designed by the group leader and will be available to all class participants. Along with this workbook, an attractive package stressing the importance of history, both Bass family history and black history, will be available.

Workshop 8: My Family/Linkage Line

Children ages five to seven years old are taught their link to Sam and Amelia Bass through stories, puzzles, arts and crafts. A take-home booklet will be given to all class members.

SUNDAY MORNING FAREWELL

If a local family member is a preacher, the group may attend church services at his or her church. Breakfast is usually on your own. Other reunions have a farewell breakfast or brunch and bring in a minister to conduct a brief morning service. Still others end their program Saturday night and Sunday breakfast is on your own.

Everything is done.
Everyone's arrived.
Everybody's eating hearty.
And now we can do
What we all love most . . .
Party, party, party!

SHOW TIME

It's show time! All the work and effort now culminates in the weekend event. As conductor it's your responsiblity to keep the beat to ensure your family harmonizes together. Of course, there's still plenty to do on reunion day. Be sure you have a reunion team in place. You'll need people to handle registration, equipment, signs and greeting guests.

REGISTRATION

Have a registration desk set up so those arriving at the reunion have a place to check in and to get all necessary information. The registration desk should be set up the evening before the reunion starts and the morning of the first day. If a picnic is the first activity, then the registration desk could be set up at the picnic site.

The registration team should have a written list of registrants and blank forms for folks registering on-site. The team gives out the registration packets, T-shirts and hats. This team should consist of friendly and smiling people. They are usually the first to meet the road-weary travelers.

Registration is the best time to get family information. Check your written list of registrants, and confirm the address and phone number of each person. Update the list as you go along.

I come from a large family, which is now five generations strong, counting from my grandparents to the youngest members of my family tree. At my last reunion, I didn't know the names of most of my first cousins once removed (first cousins' children) who were under age ten. Now I even have a bunch of cousins twice removed (children of cousins once removed). And believe me, I was not the only family member who didn't have a clue which child belonged to which cousin.

So at registration, I've started collecting the names of both the parents and their children. My goal for the next reunion is to have every child in the fourth and fifth generation named and photographed. I'm asking the parents to send me a copy of their most recent school photos.

Registration is also a good time to get a list of all the kids' names and ages. Include those both living and deceased.

Registration Packets

Registration packets contain information each person attending the reunion needs to know. Get large 8¹/2″ × 11″ or 9″ × 12″ envelopes from an office supply store. Manila or white are the least expensive, but color envelopes are available and add a dash of pizzazz. Put the name of the person who preregistered on the envelope and put all the envelopes in alphabetical order. If a person registered a family of five everything may not fit in one packet. If you are giving separate packets for spouse and children, simply staple the packets together. Most packets contain a mix of the following:

- Agenda for the weekend activities
- Materials from tourism boards
- Donations from corporations
- T-shirt if ordered in advance
- Maps to the picnic or banquet site

- Name tags
- Meal tickets
- Family update form so members can add new births, deaths, achievements and so on that happened since the last reunion

HOSPITALITY/GET-ACQUAINTED EVENING

Greeters are people who welcome visitors with a smile and a hug when they visit the hospitality event. Relatives, particularly from out-of-town, may not know most people in the room. It is the greeters' job to find out the names and relationship of the people as they walk through the door. The greeters then become icebreakers by introducing the newcomers to other family members. Just making a simple introduction such as, "This is Julian, Aunt Harriett's grandson. He came in from Detroit to be with us this weekend," will give the folks in the room plenty to build on for conversation.

The hospitality room should include food, at the minimum hors d'oeuvres, snacks and soft drinks. Most reunion planners have relatives in the host city bring food. Depending on the budget it can also include an open or cash bar. A word of caution is, however, in order. If the hospitality suite is in a hotel, you may prefer to have the hotel cater the event. See the section on liability in chapter 5 for details.

Greeters are a good idea at picnics too. When I arrived at a recent reunion, my six-year-old cousin was greeting family members with a great big hug. That really helped set the spirit of the day!

PICNIC

Make sure all family members have a ride to the picnic site. Anyone who needs one should stop at the registration desk to be put in a car pool. Have a person assigned to coordinate rides to the picnic. Encourage family members to wear their T-shirts to the reunion.

FAMILY MEETING

If your family is an incorporated family group, plan a set time to hold the annual corporate meeting. This is the opportunity to discuss any family business.

Suzanne Stantley's family, the Stanley/Harris family, has been holding family reunions for over 50 years. This family incorporated and formed a family association now known as the United Christian Family. Stantley states, "After the picnic we have a family meeting. We discuss family business and who is assigned to do whatever needs to be done in the upcoming year. We have a large reunion with over 300 people attending. Our reunion rotates from city to city. Each city has a godfather or godmother who is the head of the family in that city. The godparents make up the board of the directors."

Besides after the picnic, Sunday morning before brunch is also a good time to conduct a family meeting.

BANQUET NIGHT

You've already established your theme, and the program has been set. Before participants arrive at the banquet, place an evening agenda on each chair.

One way to distribute prizes is to randomly select one chair at each table and tape a chip, envelope or something under the seat. During the banquet announce that the person with the taped item under his or her chair has won something.

The banquet is also an opportunity to showcase family talent. If there are singers, dancers, poets or musicians in the family, have them perform. This is the time to let their light shine.

Include the children in the event. Let them give the welcome speech or say a poem or have a teen introduce the keynote speaker. It will give the youngsters confidence to speak in public.

AWARDS

Many reunions have an award ceremony as part of the banquet event. Awards are given to the oldest family members, the organizing committee chairperson and relatives who have done something deserving merit, such as recent graduates. Some reunions give away awards to the persons who had the shortest or longest distance to travel, who've been married the longest, who are new grandparents or great-grandparents, and who have the largest and smallest family groupings.

FASHION SHOW

A fashion show is a popular reunion activity. Family members model the clothes. Most reunion planners ask a local store to loan its clothes for modeling. The show promotes the store, and if the store managers are wise they'll include discount coupons to be given away at the event. If the clothes are sold at the reunion, a percentage of the sales generally go to reunion proceeds.

DANCE/PARTY

After the formal portion of the banquet, there is often a party. Family members can continue to mingle, dance, play cards and have a great time until the wee hours of the morning. If your banquet is not held at the hotel, consider having a hotel hospitality suite open for after-banquet mingling.

INTRODUCTIONS

Some reunions include a segment for introductions of all family members attending the banquet. Depending on the size of the reunion this can take some time. One idea is to go from table to table and have each person give his or her name, age (if a child), hometown, occupation, and a brief comment.

Stantley says, "My family has a big introduction segment. Each person stands with their mother and/or father. So you end up with family groups and it's easy to see which children are connected with whom. For example, my brother, sister and I get with my mother. The grandchildren get with their parents and everyone is introduced. My mother says, 'I'm Grace and these are my kids.' Then each person gives their name and tells what is their occupation and introduces their kids."

SUNDAY WORSHIP SERVICE/FAREWELL BREAKFAST

We are a spiritual people and giving honor to God is often part of the reunion experience. Sunday morning worship service is an opportunity to thank God for preserving our family, allowing us to be together yet another year and to request safe passage home.

If your group will be attending church services outside the hotel, be sure you've included a map with directions to the church and include the starting time of the worship service. Be sure to let everyone know if a dress code applies. There are still many churches in African-American communities that don't want women to wear pants to services.

Family members can also conduct morning prayer or worship service at breakfast. This can be a time to honor ancestors and remember the deceased.

Many reunions ask a nonfamily clergy member to conduct service at the morning brunch. If this is the case, have the agreed-upon honorarium ready at the close of the morning event.

Some farewell breakfasts are casual and unstructured. Folks have breakfast on their own or can sleep in if they prefer.

EVALUATION

Pass out a reunion evaluation form. This is an opportunity to get feedback from participants about what they liked and didn't like about the reunion. Keep the form short and easy to fill out. (See the sample evaluation form.)

It is important to get the evaluations filled out before people head home. It is almost impossible to get them to fill out the forms when they get back to their hectic lives.

CLOSING OUT THE DETAILS

Be sure to close out your final hotel bill. At that time get all the information you can about how many rooms were rented and how many meals were served at each event and through room service. Remember, it is important to establish a history for your reunions. You want to get an understanding of the financial impact your reunion has on a hotel. This is essential for future negotiations.

Also, return any borrowed equipment and take down all signs.

FAREWELL

It's been a blast! But now it's time to say good-bye. The last day of a reunion is filled with tears, hugs, exchanging phone numbers and promises to stay in touch. You and the reunion committee can take pride in a job well done. This is a gift you have given your family that it will always treasure.

More than that, you may never know the impact the reunion had on those who attended. Perhaps a fence has been mended

EVALUATION FORM

Thank you for attending this year's reunion. We appreciate your participation. We'd like our reunions to get better each year. Please help by taking a few minutes to complete this form. Give us any comments about what you liked and didn't like. We'd also appreciate any suggestions for next year. Please turn in your completed evaluation as you leave. All information is strictly confidential.

1. How many reunions have you attended? _____

2. How were the hotel accommodations?
   Poor   Fair   Good   Great

3. How were the hotel meals?
   Poor   Fair   Good   Great

4. The program book was
   Poor   Fair   Good   Great

5. Reunion organization was
   Poor   Fair   Good   Great

6. What is your sex and age?   Male _____   Female _____
   Under 12   13–19   20–40   41–60   60+

7. What did you like most about the reunion?

   _____

   _____

   _____

8. What did you like least about the reunion?

   _____

   _____

   _____

9. Are you planning on attending the next reunion?
   Sure   Very likely   Not at this time

10. Give us your comments/ideas for upcoming reunions. (Use the back side for more comments and ideas.)

   _____

   _____

   _____

making way for forgiveness. Perhaps two distant cousins got a chance to get acquainted and found a common bond. Perhaps a new romance has sparked between an invited guest and a family member. Perhaps sharing the family history has instilled pride in a child. Actually, reunions are more than a gift—they're part of your family's legacy.

Let's remember the fun,
Remember the love,
Cherish every smile,
Hug and tear.
And as our family grows older
Our memories will grow dearer
Year after year after year.

PRESERVING FAMILY HISTORY

Capturing and preserving the fun and spirit of your family reunion in words, pictures and videos create a priceless collection to be shared for years to come. This collection can be displayed at future reunions, and will be passed down from generation to generation. As a practicing genealogist, I encourage you to also use your family reunion to collect and preserve your family's history and heritage. Once the information has been gathered, reunions are a time to share this rich history and to create a sense of family and cultural pride.

What you are seeking to capture is both the history (the actual family facts, such as names, dates, places and so on) and the heritage (your family's story, tales, life experiences, traditions and so on). Collecting oral history is one of the best ways to get information to develop your family's story.

ORAL HISTORY

The oral story tradition was passed down from African ancestors and is still practiced today. Most African villages are large family compounds made up of several generations. The villages are usually named after the family who lives there. In each village there is a griot whose responsibility it is to memorize the genealogy and history of the village to ensure that it is passed down from one generation to the next. Most griots can tell a village's history back many generations. This tradition was carried through during the period of slavery. Since most slaves could neither read nor write stories about plantation life were passed on orally. By conducting oral interviews you'll be keeping this tradition alive in your own family.

This chapter, then, is about the past, the present and the future. You are going back to the past, picking up the strings of time and weaving them with the reunions of the present. This creates a rich tapestry of your family's struggles and triumphs, to share with one another today, and to preserve for generations yet unborn.

Collecting your family history and preserving your reunion history is a fun part of the reunion experience. After all, today's reunion will soon be history, so be sure to capture the highlights. Who wouldn't want to see little five-year-old Henry giving the welcome speech, or seventy-year-old Aunt Edith strutting her stuff in the fashion show, or the newly ordained reverend (Uncle Joe) giving his first public sermon at the reunion, or cousin David's impression of Little Richard in the talent show? These are priceless moments that create lasting memories. How you can preserve those memories is the focus of this chapter.

COLLECTING FAMILY HISTORY AND HERITAGE

I am not trying to turn you into a genealogist. For that, you'll need to read my book *Family Pride: The Complete Guide to Tracing African-American Genealogy*. What I do want to do here is give you some basic steps you can take at a family reunion to begin capturing your family's history and heritage. This is a busy time for all attendees, and you don't want to distract them from the fun too long. But you or someone from the committee should take on the job of gathering the information. Whoever does this becomes in essence the reunion griot or family historian. To keep it simple, take a two-step approach.

Get the Facts

The first step in recording your family history is to develop a family tree. At a reunion, normally one or two family lines are the focus. You want to gather the facts of those lines—names, dates, places and relationships. If you ever want to expand to a full genealogical search, this will be the foundation on which you build your family's genealogy.

Before you or your appointed griot gets to the reunion, you should gather as many facts as you can. Start with yourself—you are the beginning twig on your family tree. Begin with how you are connected to the family and work backward. You want to start with the known and work your way back to the unknown ancestors. So you would list your name, your parents' names, grandparents' names, great-grandparents' names and so on. At some point you won't be able to go any further—this is the unknown information.

Next, check all resources available at home, such as birth certificates, marriage licenses, family bibles, scrapbooks and so on. Gather all the information you can. Soon you'll have an idea of what you have and what information you need.

Next, try to fill as many information gaps as you can by talking to people at the reunion. Find out where the family originally came from, favorite family traditions, where various members grew up, what kind of work they do and the names of their immediate family members. Take notes as you go along. Once you talk to several people you'll have an idea of who are the most knowledgeable members of the family. These are the people you focus on for the second step.

Oral Interviews

The purpose of collecting oral history is to move beyond the facts of your genealogy to develop your family's heritage. You don't just want to list names and dates, because your history will be boring to read. Remember, your purpose is to create a family keepsake that can be shared from reunion to reunion. Plus, this can be an ongoing project where people add a little more to the family's heritage each year.

When conducting your oral interviews you may be surprised that two people telling the same story will remember it differently. It's okay; this is normal. A person's age, frame of mind and how personally he or she was affected, all play a role in how a person remembers the past. It is each individual's interpretation you want to capture. It is impossible to document a person's life in an hour-long interview. But it is a wonderful snapshot into that person's life.

Always interview the eldest relatives first, and then move on to those who seem to have the most knowledge. Prepare a list of questions before the reunion or at the very least, before the interview. In addition to the facts, you want to capture life experiences. The key is to note both the details of the family history and the spirit of the family heritage. What were their accomplishments or disappointments? What was it like growing up in their home or neighborhood? What were their parents, brothers and sisters like? What memories do they have of their grandparents? What were holidays like? These are the kinds of questions that give you insight into a person's life experiences.

Many relatives may feel they've done nothing in their lives worth discussing. Assure these reluctant relatives you are not seeking great historical events. You just want to know what their lives were like growing up. Assure them there are no right or wrong answers. Ask them to take a stroll with you down memory lane. Begin with childhood memories and soon they'll warm up and get into the spirit of the interview.

Equipment Needs

A tape recorder and notepad are the tools of the trade for collecting oral interviews. Tape recorders are best because they free you up to participate in the discussion. But remember, you are there to listen and guide the interviewee—not to dominate the conversation. Always take a notepad. I've done many interviews that were supposed to be two hours that went for four hours. The pad is a backup in case you run out of tape before your interview ends. Plus, it makes sense to write down a person's name, date of birth, marriage date and names of children, parents and grandparents on the pad. That way you don't have to transcribe the tape to get this information.

Be sure you test the recorder before your interview. You don't want to finish your session and discover the batteries were dead. Also, eliminate all the background noises you can. Television or radio chatter can make it a nightmare to transcribe the tape later.

PHOTOGRAPHS

"A picture is worth a thousand words" is an old cliché, but so true. Looking at old photographs opens the flood gates to memories of pleasurable events and unforgettable loved ones. Don't miss the great photo opportunities at your reunion. Be sure to take a camera. Make sure someone on the reunion committee is responsible for capturing candid shots.

Most people take color pictures at reunions. For long-term preservation, however, it is important to take a few rolls of black and white pictures. These photos can last for over 100 years. Color photos have a life span of about 50 years. This means the color snapshots you take of the newborn twins this reunion may not be around to show at the twins' retirement party when they reach age sixty-five.

Caring for Photographs

Photographs are a historic resource and need proper care and storage. Do not use photo albums you can purchase in discount stores to preserve your family's photo history. The albums may actually be harmful to your photographs by causing them to fade and discolor over time. The best and safest route is to use high-quality, acid-free, photo-safe albums, folders and sleeves. These use acid-free paper.

These photo-safe albums can be purchased at art supply stores. You can also order them via direct mail from the following two sources.

Light Impressions
439 Monroe Ave.
P.O. Box 940
Rochester, NY 14603
(800) 828-9859

Gaylord Bros.
P.O. Box 4901
Syracuse, NY 13221
(800) 428-9859

Professional Photographer

Consider hiring a professional photographer for a full day during the reunion. This person's job is to take pictures of small family groups. Uncle Henry, his wife, children and grandchildren make up a small family group. These shots can be taken inside or outside at the picnic. Thirty minutes before the banquet, or right after all the small family shots are taken, is a great time to take a group photo of the whole family. A professional photographer will know how to arrange the group so all the faces are captured on film. You want to be careful that someone's face is not hidden by someone else's head.

Depending on the size of your reunion, the photographer may also have time to capture picnic or banquet highlights as he or she mingles with the crowd. Obviously there is a fee to hire a professional photographer. Shop around to get a good deal.

If a professional photographer is not in your budget, don't fret. An amateur photographer with a good camera can work out just fine. Also, ask relatives who are taking photos to make a duplicate set and send them to you. Do not save every photo you receive. Take the best of each bunch for preservation and forward the rest on for the enjoyment of relatives who missed the reunion.

VIDEO

Video cameras are showing up at more reunions. This is an excellent way to capture the memories. It is also a good way to preserve your family's heritage. If your reunion is a weekend event, ask a few of the older family members and knowledgeable younger members if they would let you interview them on camera. Most will respond positively. Some won't do it alone, but will do it in a two- or three-person group setting. So you may get a husband and wife or two brothers to interview together. Once they start traveling down memory lane, one person's comments will spark the thoughts of the other to create a wonderful session.

The purpose of this is to capture on video the faces, voices and comments of these relatives. No photograph can freeze for all posterity the voice, laughter, mannerisms and view of life that can be captured on video. The beauty of placing it on film is that later the interviews can be mixed with photographs and memorabilia to create your own family documentary.

I am in the midst of creating my own family video documentary as I write this book. My mother is one of twenty children. There are only four siblings still living. They are the matriarchs of the family, and I felt capturing them and their comments about family life would be an invaluable addition to our family heritage. Plus, the addition of live footage would add life and vibrancy to the still photos and stories I've collected over the years. I was also fortunate enough to have audiotaped many of the sisters and brothers before they passed on. I can include their actual voices over their individual and family photos as they discuss their lives.

I interviewed two of the siblings or my mom and her sister at the last family reunion. (The other two aunts did not attend.) My family has a picnic each year, so I set up a table away from the reunion site and did the interviews. Doing an interview at an outdoor picnic does have its challenges. For instance, I had to ask the deejay not to play music for thirty minutes. And being near the airport, we occasionally had to stop for noisy airplanes flying overhead. But I got the interviews. During that same reunion I also got some great group shots on film. I'll interview my other two aunts separately, and then I will intersperse the video footage, audio interviews, photographs and our family story to create a keepsake video documentary. You can do it too. Here's how.

CREATING A VIDEO DOCUMENTARY
Hire a Professional
You can hire a professional videographer for the day. He or she can do select interviews with family members throughout the day. In between interviews, this same videographer can get some great candid shots. Every effort should be made to get everyone who attends the reunion in the video.

After the reunion bring your photographs and memorabilia to the videographer. Be as organized as possible. Videographers generally charge $30 to $50 per hour. You don't want to pay them to do stuff you can do yourself, like put your photos in order. Also, write out your family's story and have someone recite it for the videographer. He or she will then videotape and edit together all the elements to create the keepsake video.

Do It Yourself
Grandmother Mary Lou Peterson was in charge of entertaining the children at her family reunion. The previous year she had

organized volleyball and softball games, but she wanted something different for this year. At Christmas she transferred her home movies to videotape, and her children loved it. "So," states Peterson, "I took my family tree book and put together a story. I got a storyteller to do the narration and created a twenty-minute video documentary. It was a hit at the family reunion.

"I told the attending family, if you like, we can take this one step further next year. If you send in your photographs I'll put them on video. We'll have our story in both book and video form. The reunion was in August and over the next couple of months the photos poured in. By December, I had everything on video. More importantly, my family had a wonderful keepsake video documentary that brings our family tree to life."

Peterson, a video novice, couldn't find any resources to guide her through the development of her family project. So to help other reunion planners, she took everything she learned and created an information-packed instructional videotape called the "Gift of Heritage." The videotape takes the viewer through the process of beginning the research, planning and organizing materials and combining family tree information, photographs, slides and home movie and video footage to effectively tell your story. If you are interested in creating a family video keepsake, consider getting Peterson's video. It is full of helpful tips and ideas, and it is sure to take the fear and frustration out of the process.

Mary Lou Peterson
Gift of Heritage
P.O. Box 17233
Minneapolis, MN 55417
(800) 774-8511

REUNION PROGRAM BOOKLET

Many reunions planners create a keepsake program booklet. In it are a variety of things including a welcome letter from the planning committee, poems, puzzles, a family address directory, family facts and similar information. Two of the most popular poems used in African-American program booklets are "Family Pledge" by Maya Angelou and "What Shall I Tell My Children Who Are Black" by Dr. Margaret Burroughs.

Strive to make your program booklet go beyond being fun and entertaining by using it as a tool to build family pride and preserve your family's history. The booklet is a wonderful place to add a story on how the family reunion got started and to provide the story of the ancestors from whom you're descended.

Making Booklets

Type up and gather all the information that is going into the program booklet. This is called your copy and visuals (puzzles, photos and so on). Be sure the information is written in a clear, easy-to-understand manner. Have at least two people read all the copy to be sure there are no typos or other errors.

Next, you want to make the copy as visually interesting as possible. For example, you may center a poem on the paper and surround it with a pretty border. One reunion planner wrote a wonderful welcome letter and next to her signature she placed a small photo of herself, adding a personal feel to the letter.

Take extra care in planning your cover. It should include the theme, if you have one, the family name and the reunion city. It also should be visually interesting. You can create interest by manipulating type sizes and fonts or by using clip art as discussed in chapter 3.

Once the information is organized and the cover complete you are ready to have the pages duplicated. Head for a quick copy shop like Kinkos or Speedy Print. Make enough copies for the expected number of attendees plus 10 to 20 percent extra for last-minute check-ins or for people who'd like an extra copy.

Have the copy shop bind the booklet with a spiral binding or staples. Pick a card stock for the front and back cover of the book.

Card stock is heavier than regular paper, and will protect the interior pages. You can choose from a variety of colors.

Remember to include the cost of making the booklets in your reunion budget. The copy shop can help you work out a budget estimate in the early planning stages.

We've had fun, food and love
And shared memories galore.
This year's reunion was
Better than before.
Now, it's time to say goodbye
With a smile and a tear.
Knowing we'll all be
Together again next year.

THE FINALE

In your lifetime your family has given you many gifts, the greatest of which is love. Planning and hosting a family reunion, and preserving your family's heritage, are love gifts you give back to your family. Tom Ninkovich, founder of Reunion Research and author of the *Family Reunion Handbook,* says it best: "Reunions are probably the most social event in our society, at least as far as positive social impact goes. I've interviewed over 3,000 reunion planners and I'm still amazed at the stories I hear—on how reunions have helped change people and families for the better. That's why it's important to make your reunion the best it can be. Future generations will thank you more than you can know."

ADDITIONAL SUPPORT SYSTEMS

If you need additional help or just want to network with other reunion planners, consider joining a genealogy club or attending a genealogy conference. Many genealogists are their family griots or historians, and often play a prominent role in planning the family reunion. In fact, genealogists are often the founders of their family's reunion. A list of genealogy clubs is included in the appendix of this book. These clubs are also a good source for getting a keynote speaker for a reunion banquet.

A genealogy conference can provide both hands-on training and networking opportunities. Dr. Ione Vargas, professor emeritus, founded the Family Reunion Institute at Temple University. It organizes and conducts the African-American Reunion Conference. Dr. Vargas says, "We have eight or nine workshops during each conference to train reunion planners. Seminar topics usually include how to plan a family reunion, how to trace your roots, how to tell your history and how to preserve documents, to name a few.

"We've held the conference in Philadelphia for the past nine years but we will be taking it around the country in future years."

For more information on the conference, contact:

Family Reunion Institute
School of Social Administration
Temple University
Philadelphia, PA 19122
215-204-6244

The Reunion Network is another organization that conducts workshops to train reunion planners. Sometimes the Network sponsors planning trips to certain U.S. cities to check out the various hotels and facilities available. These trips help promote tourism in the city by encouraging you to host your reunion there. The Reunion Network also offers problem-solving assistance. It may be able to help you if you have a major problem with your reunion and don't know what to do. For example, if your hotel has overbooked and you need to find rooms for eighty traveling family members in three days, the Reunion Network may be able to offer assistance. Be sure to ask about its fees.

The Reunion Network, Inc.
2450 Hollywood Blvd. Suite 301
Hollywood, FL 33020
954-922-0004

"Reunions are the ultimate family ritual," proclaims Edith Wagner, publisher of *Reunions Magazine*. "Reunions build tradition, create memories, strengthen families and are celebrations of hope. Every phase of human existence comes into play at family reunions. Milestones, accomplishments, honors, kudos and accolades are celebrated and everyone feels proud that this is, 'my stock . . . my blood . . . where I came from. These are my people.' [It is] a pride of belonging.

"Reunions provide opportunities to recall, relive, be nostalgic and wax eloquent. For older members, reunions are an opportunity to pass 'it' along and if the younger ones have any brains at all, they'll soak it up—storytellers, griots, history weavers."

Reunions Magazine is a great source of information on what has worked for others and an outlet for sharing your reunion experience. This quarterly journal is a cornucopia of ideas and suggestions for enhancing your reunion.

Reunions Magazine
P.O. Box 11727
Milwaukee, WI 53211-0727
414-263-4567
E-mail: Reunions@execpc.com
Web Page: http://www.execpc.com/~reunions

Reunion Research is a company that publishes information useful to reunion planners and others interested in the reunion market. Statistical information is also available.

Reunion Research
3145 Geary Blvd., #14
San Francisco, CA 94118
209-855-2101

We've reached the finale. In all family reunions there comes a time to say tearful good-byes as our family members "case on down the road" of life. Throughout this book, you've orchestrated the family reunion, gotten great teamwork from the family rhythm section, celebrated every family member from the youngest bongo to the oldest drum and preserved your heritage for future generations. You arrived at the reunion crescendo organized and confident, and graciously accepted hard-earned kudos at the final curtain call. Congratulations on a job well done.

Now that your successful reunion is over it's time to stop and exhale. Stand in front of the mirror and pat yourself on the back. As the conductor of a fabulous family symphony, take a well-deserved bow. Bravo!

Appendixes

Printers

If you are interested in creating a family cookbook, these printers can help:

Cookbook Publishers Inc.
10800 Lakeview Ave.
Lenexa, KS 66219
800-227-7282

Walter's Cookbooks
215 5th Avenue SE
Waseca, MN 56093
800-447-3274

African-American Historical and Genealogical Societies

Many different types of organizations are listed here. The National Afro-American Historical and Genealogical Society (AAHGS), headquartered in Washington, D.C., has many affiliates and chapters throughout the United States. These AAHGS affiliates are so noted. These genealogical organizations are an excellent resource for keynote speakers.

AAHGS— U.S. National Headquarters

Afro-American Historical and
  Genealogical Society, Inc.
1700 Shepherd St. N.W.
Washington, DC 20011

Arizona

AAHGS—Tucson
P.O. Box 58272
Tucson, AZ 87554

Buffalo Soldiers Historical Society, Inc.
324 W. Aspen
P.O. Box 937
Flagstaff, AZ 86001

California

Afro-American Genealogical Society
600 State Dr.
Exposition Park
Los Angeles, CA 90037

Black Military History Society
1793 Coary St.
San Francisco, CA 94115

Canada

Black Cultural Centre for
Nova Scotia
P.O. Box 2128 East Dartmouth
Nova Scotia B2W 3Y2 Canada

Colorado

The Black Genealogy Search Group
P.O. Box 40674
Denver, CO 80204-0674

Florida

AAHGS—Central Florida
P.O. Box 5742
Deltona, FL 32728

Georgia

African-American Family History
Association
C2077 Bent Creek Way SW
Atlanta, GA 30311

Illinois

AAHGS—Little Egypt
703 S. Wall St., #5
Carbondale, IL 62901

AAHGS—Patricia Liddell
Researchers
P.O. Box 438652
Chicago, IL 60643

Afro-American Genealogical
and Historical Society
of Chicago
P.O. Box 37-7651
Chicago, IL 60637

Indiana

Indiana African-American Historical
and Genealogical Society
502 Clover Terrace
Bloomington, IN 47404-1809

Louisiana

Afro-Louisiana Historical and
Genealogical Society
P.O. Box 2247
Baton Rouge, LA 70821

Maryland

AAHGS—Central Maryland
P.O. Box 2774
Columbia, MD 21045

AAHGS—Prince Georges County
P.O. Box 447772
Ft. Washington, MD 20744-9998

Michigan

Fred Hart Williams Genealogical
Society
Burton Historical Collection
5201 Woodward Ave.
Detroit, MI 48202

Missouri

AAHGS—Landon Cheek
P.O. Box 23804
St. Louis, MO 63121-0840

AAHGS—MAGIC
3700 Blue Parkway
Kansas City, MO 64130

New Jersey

AAHGS—New Jersey
785 Sterling Dr. East
South Orange, NJ 07079

New York

AAHGS—JSS Greater New York
P.O. Box 022340
Brooklyn, NY 11201

North Carolina

Afro-American Family History Project
P.O. Box 6074
Greensboro, NC 27405

North Carolina Afro-American
  Heritage Society
P.O. 26334
Raleigh, NC 27611

Ohio

African-American Genealogical
  Society of Cleveland
P.O. Box 200382
Cleveland, OH 44120

Pennsylvania

AAHGS—Western Pennsylvania
P-1832 Runnette St.
Pittsburgh, PA 15235

African-American Genealogy
  Group
P.O. Box 1798
Philadelphia, PA 19105

Rhode Island

Rhode Island Black Heritage
  Society
46 Aborn St.
Providence, RI 02903

Tennessee

African-American Genealogical
  and Historical Society
P.O. Box 17684
Nashville, TN 37217

Texas

AAHGS—Houston
P.O. Box 750877
Houston, TX 77275-0877

Tarrant County Black History and
  Genealogical Society
1020 E. Humboldt
Fort Worth, TX 76104

Virginia

AAHGS—Hampton Roads
P.O. Box 2448
Newport News, VA 23609

AAHGS—Tidewater Chapter
2200 Crossroad Trail
Virginia Beach, VA 23456

Washington, D.C.

AAHGS, D.C.—James Dent Walker
P.O. Box 34683
Washington, DC 20043

TRAVEL AND TOURISM INFORMATION

CITY TOURISM BUREAUS

Cultural Center
77 East Randolph Street
Chicago, Illinois 60602
312-744-2400

African American COE-Cleveland
50 Public Square
Suite 3100
Cleveland, OH 44113
800-282-5393

Detroit Bureau of Tourism
100 Renaissance Center
Suite 126
Detroit, MI 48243
800-DETROIT

Jackson Mississippi Bureau of Tourism
P.O. Box 849
Jackson, MS 39205-0849
800-927-6378

Parks Tourist Bureau
One Capital Mall
Little Rock, AR 72201
800-628-8725

Convention & Visitors Bureau
685 South Figueroa Street
Los Angeles, CA 90017
213-624-7300

Bureau of Tourism
401 Adams Avenue
Suite 126
Montgomery, AL 36103
800-ALABAMA

Bureau of Tourism
1520 Sugarbowl Drive
New Orleans, LA 70112
800-633-6970

STATE TOURISM BUREAUS

D.C. Convention and Visitors Association
1212 New York Avenue, NW
Washington, DC 20005
202-789-7000

Delaware Tourism Office
99 Kings Highway
Box 1401
Dover, DE 19903
800-441-8846

APPENDIX C

Florida Division of Tourism
126 Van Buren Street
Tallahassee, FL
904-487-1462

Georgia Department of Industry
and Trade
Box 1776
Atlanta, GA 30301
800-847-4842

Illinois Travel Information
Center
c/o Department of Commerce
and Community Affairs
620 East Adams Street
Springfield, IL 62701
217-782-7139

Indiana Department of Commerce
Tourist Development Division
1 North Capitol Avenue, Suite 700
Indianapolis, IN 46204
800-289-ONIN

Kansas Department of Travel and
Tourism
700 SW Harrison
Suite 1300
Topeka, KS 66603
800-2-KANSAS

Louisiana Office of Tourism
Box 94291
Baton Rouge, LA 70804
800-33-GUMBO

Maryland Office of Tourism
Development
217 East Redwood Street
Baltimore, MD 21202
800-543-1036

Michigan Department of Commerce
Travel Bureau
Box 30226
Lansing, MI 48909
800-5432-YES

Mississippi Department of Economic
Development
Division of Tourism
P.O. Box 22825
Jackson, MS 39205-3297
800-647-2290

Missouri Division of Tourism
Truman State Office Building
Box 1055
Jefferson City, MO 65102
314-751-4133

New Jersey Office of Travel and
Tourism
CN-826
20 West State Street
Trenton, NJ 08625
800-JERSEY-7

New York Divison of Tourism
One Commerce Plaza
Albany, NY 12245
800-255-5697

North Carolina Travel and Tourism
Divison
430 North Salisbury Street
Raleigh, NC 27603
800-VISIT-NC

Ohio Department of Development
Division of Travel and Tourism
Box 1001
Columbus, OH 43266
800-BUCKEYE

Oklahoma Tourism and Recreation
  Department
P.O. Box 60000
Oklahoma City, OK 73146
800-652-6552

Pennsylvania Bureau of Travel
  Development
9 East Athens Avenue
Ardmore, PA 19003-9626
800-VISIT-PA

South Carolina Department of
  Parks, Recreation, and Tourism
1205 Pendelton Street
Columbia, SC 29201
803-734-0235

Tennessee Department of
  Tourism
Box 23170
Nashville, TN 37202
615-741-2158

Texas Travel and Information
  Division
Box 5064
Austin, TX 78763
512-483-3705

HOTELS WITH NATIONAL TOLL-FREE NUMBERS

Howard Johnson	800-654-2000	Ramada Inn	800-2-RAMADA
Hyatt	800-228-9000	Holiday Inn	800-HOLIDAY
Marriott	800-228-9280	Best Western	800-528-1234

AIRLINES WITH TOLL-FREE RESERVATION NUMBERS

US Air	800-428-4322	Northwest	800-447-4747
American Airlines	800-433-7300	TWA	800-221-2000
Continental	800-221-1212	United	800-241-6522

CRUISE INFORMATION

Cruise Director of New York	800-348-0009
Cruise Reunions	800-852-3268

Bibliography

It is difficult to find a book on reunion planning in the store. But these titles can be found in libraries or purchased direct from the publisher.

Brown, Barbara, and Tom Ninkovich. *Family Reunion Handbook— A Thorough Guide to Family Reunion Planning.* San Francisco: Reunion Research, 1992.

To order contact:

Reunion Research
3145 Geary Blvd. #14
San Francisco, CA 94118

Wisdom, Emma J. *A Practical Guide to Planning a Family Reunion.* Nashville: Post Oak Publications, 1988.

To order contact:

Post Oak Publications
P.O. Box 8455
Nashville, TN 37207

These are excellent examples of cookbooks you can review:

The Black Family Reunion Cookbook. Memphis: Wimmer Books Plus, 1991.

Black Family Dinner Quilt Cookbook. Memphis: Wimmer Books Plus, 1993.

BIBLIOGRAPHY

Celebrating Our Mothers' Kitchens. Memphis: Wimmer books Plus, 1994.

All three are released by the National Council of Negro Women. They can be found or ordered in stores, or contact the publisher:

Wimmer Books Plus
4210 B.F. Goodrich Blvd.
Memphis, TN 38118
(800) 727-1034

Index

◇